COME TO BEAUTIFUL RUSTON-

A WONDERFUL PLACE TO LIVE

by John Wood

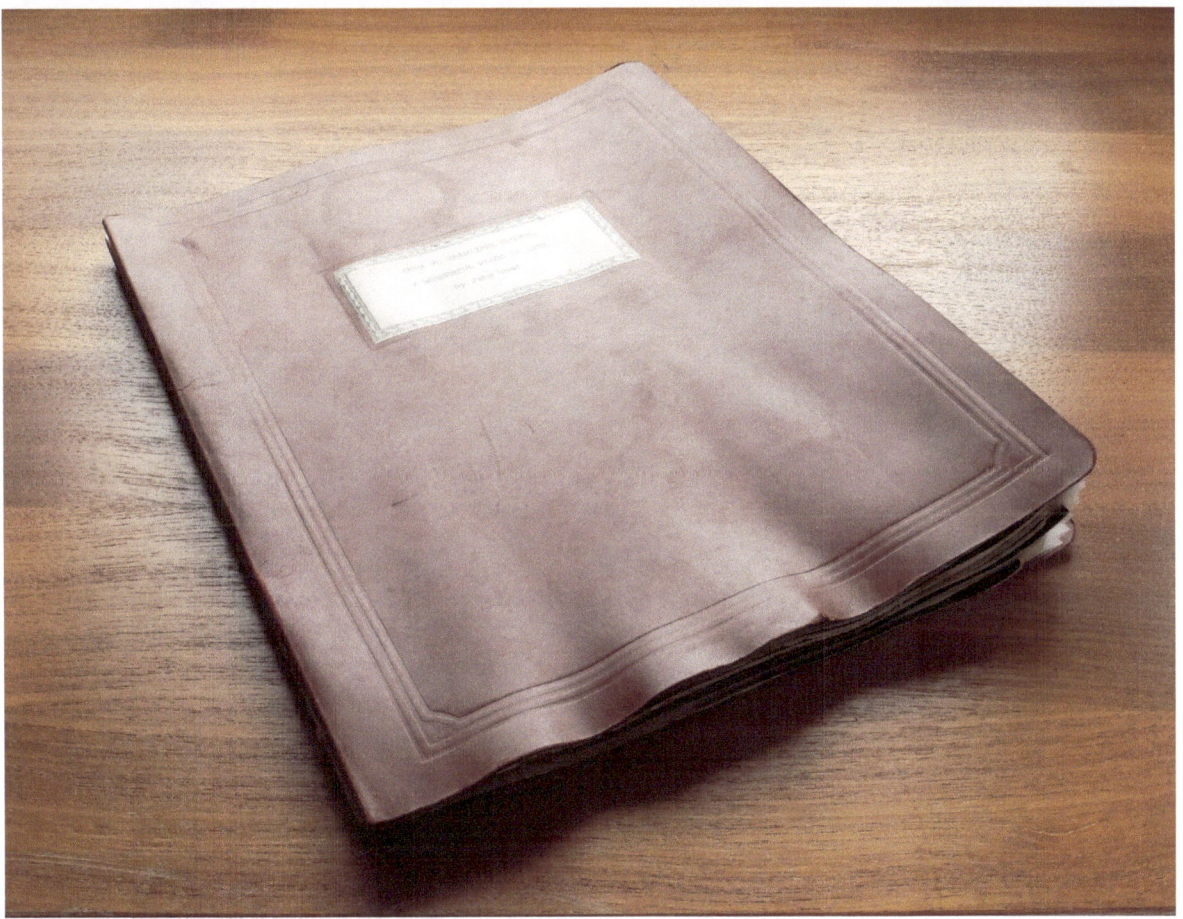

Come to Beautiful Ruston is a photographic essay about a college town in north central Louisiana. As a Louisiana Tech student from 1961 to 1965, the author worked as a photographer in the journalism department, and contributed photos to the *Lagniappe* yearbook, *Tech Talk* newspaper, *Ruston Daily Leader* newspaper and other publications.

This booklet was a one-off, a creative whim, filmed on a weekend after enlisting friends as models. After graduation the thin volume followed the author in moves from Louisiana to Texas, Massachusetts, California, Massachusetts, New Mexico, and Massachusetts. The cover gained a scar from a hot coffee cup, and the pages were wrinkled, having survived a flooded basement. Most of the time the booklet stayed on a shelf, and was occasionally taken down and examined.

As the author got older, the photograph's captions seemed increasingly sophomoric, and downright cynical – the product of a bored student poking fun at a quite-nice college town. Then one day he realized the booklet was a half-century old, and that the photographs might be of interest. Surely Ruston had changed in fifty years. A few modern notes complement the photographs.

John Wood
Concord, Massachusetts
January 2015

AKNOWLEDGEMENTS

The author wishes to acknowledge the deans, professors and instructors at Louisiana Tech University for a superb educational experience. Nowadays many high school graduates are offered several choices in colleges. The author wanted to be an engineer, like his father, and was offered only one college choice – Louisiana Polytechnic Institute, as it was known at the time. He never regretted having but one option.

Thanks to Steve Rodakis for hiring the author at Tech Studio as a photographer. He was an excellent mentor in the art and practice of photography. Thanks also to Steve for assisting with the modern captions.

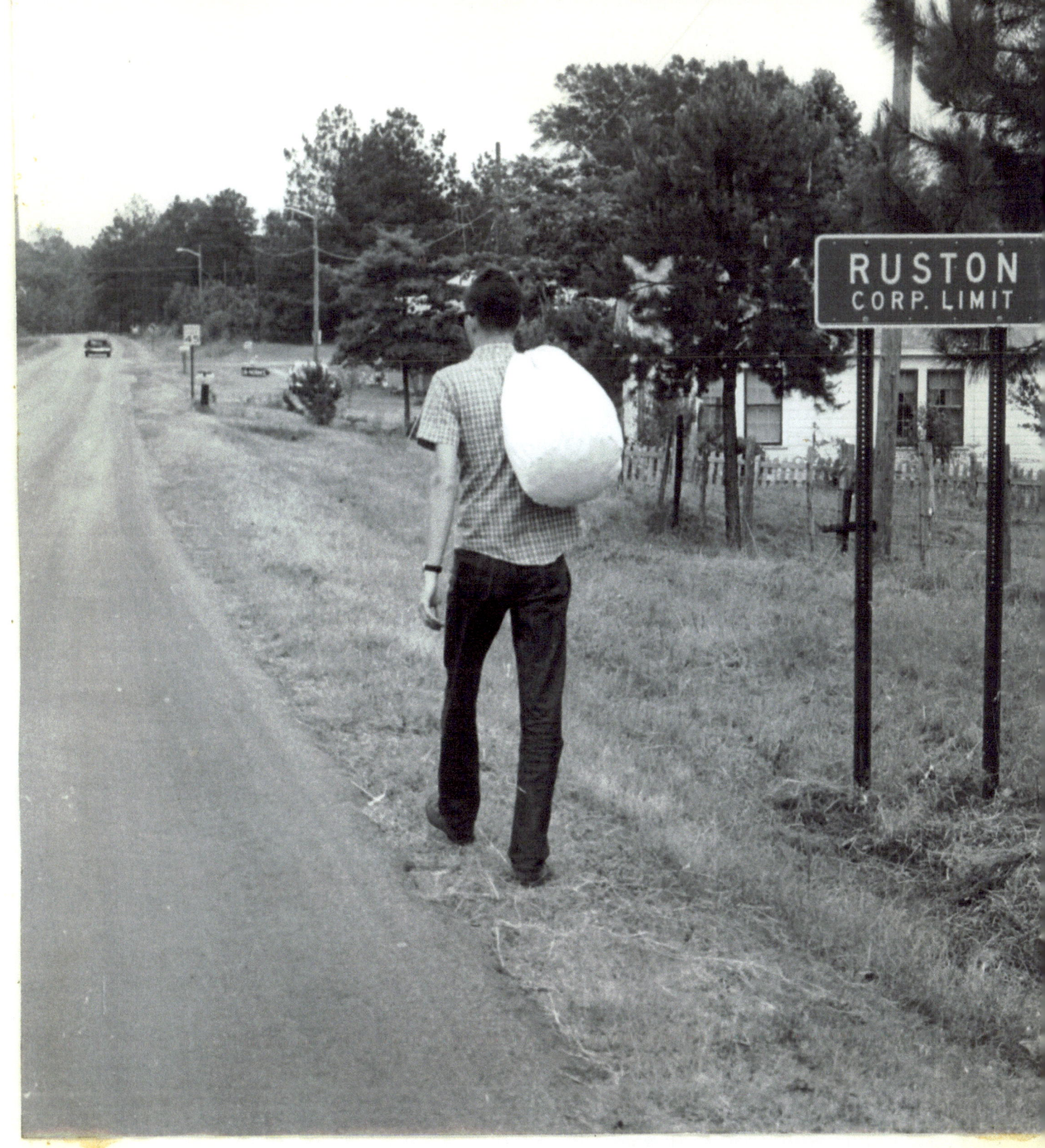

Why don't you do as this gentleman has and become one of the
thousands of people who visit Ruston each year. There is
something different about Ruston-style living - an exciting
quality about this shining modern city where the warmth of
Southern hospitality blooms.

3

Ruston's crossroads status is in jeopardy as most of this scene is now missing. This photo was made along Monroe Street, looking east down the Kansas City Southern rail line. The north/south tracks running left-to-right were removed. The train station, with its quaint hand trucks, was torn down and the area is now Railroad Park.

This photo was taken looking southwest from the roof of the T. L. James Building, which overlooks the intersection of West Mississippi Avenue and North Trenton Street. The cupola of Keeny Hall and the power plant are visible in the distance.

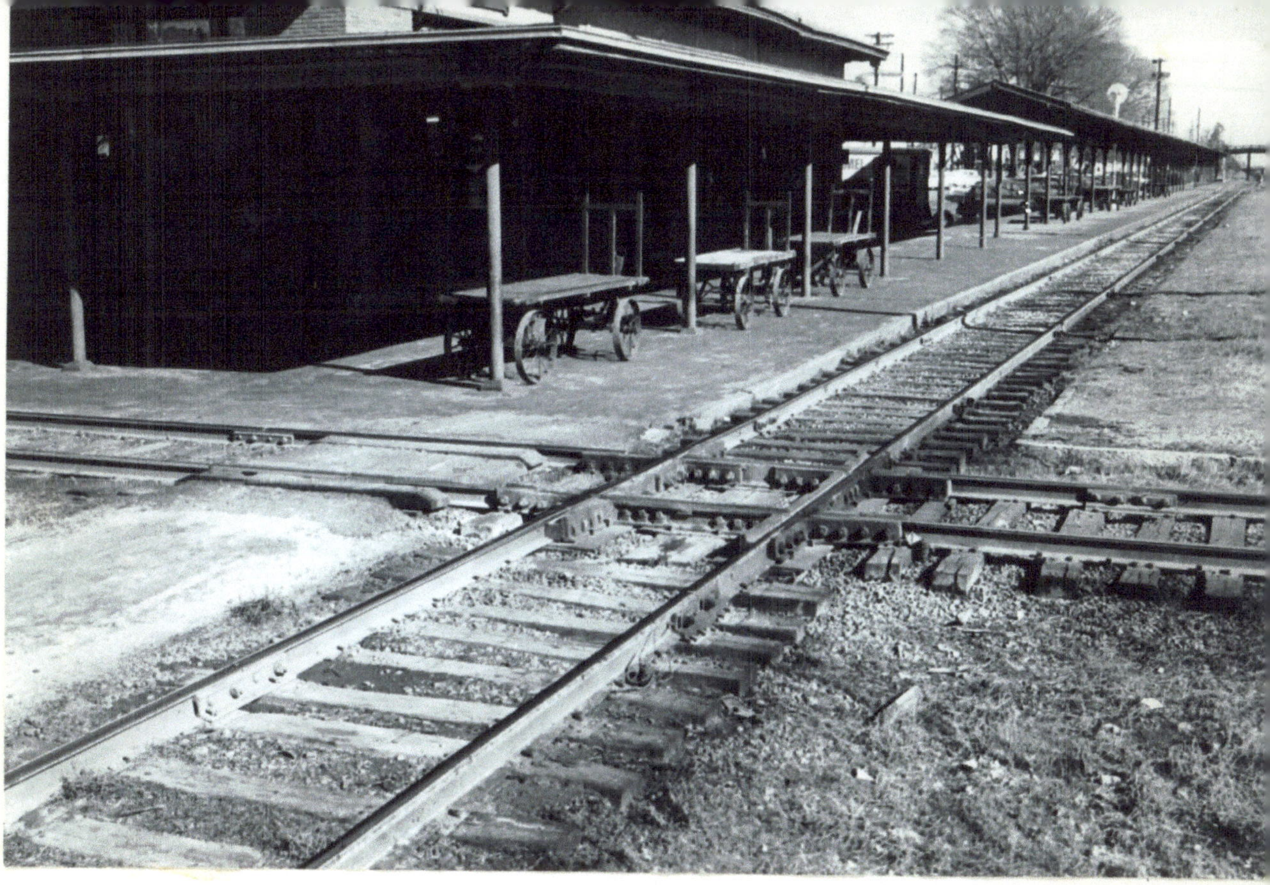

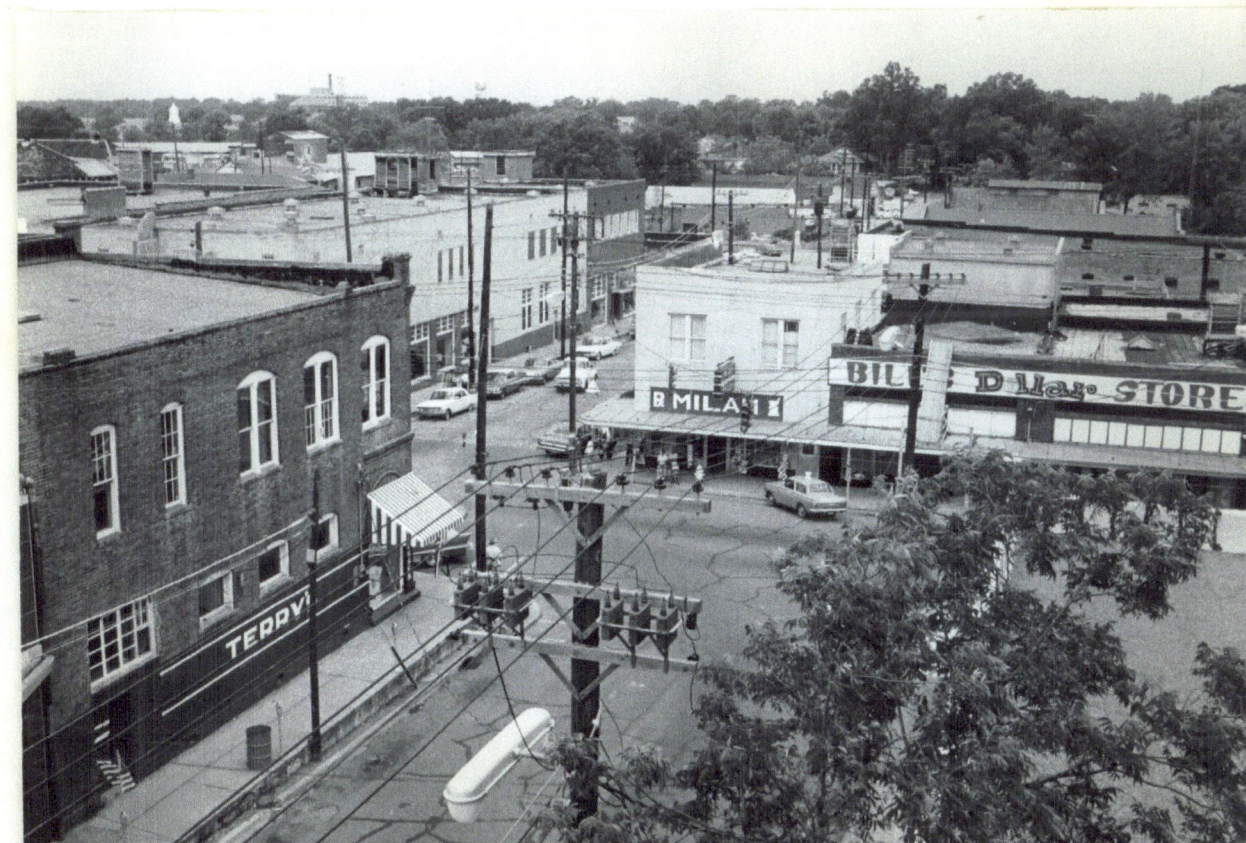

Ruston is the crossroads of the world, all activity is centered around this glittering gem nestled in the gently rolling hills of northern Louisiana.

From your first look at Ruston's breath-taking skyline you will fall in love with our fair city.

Lewis Alley runs east/west between North Vienna and North Trenton Streets, south of West Mississippi Avenue.

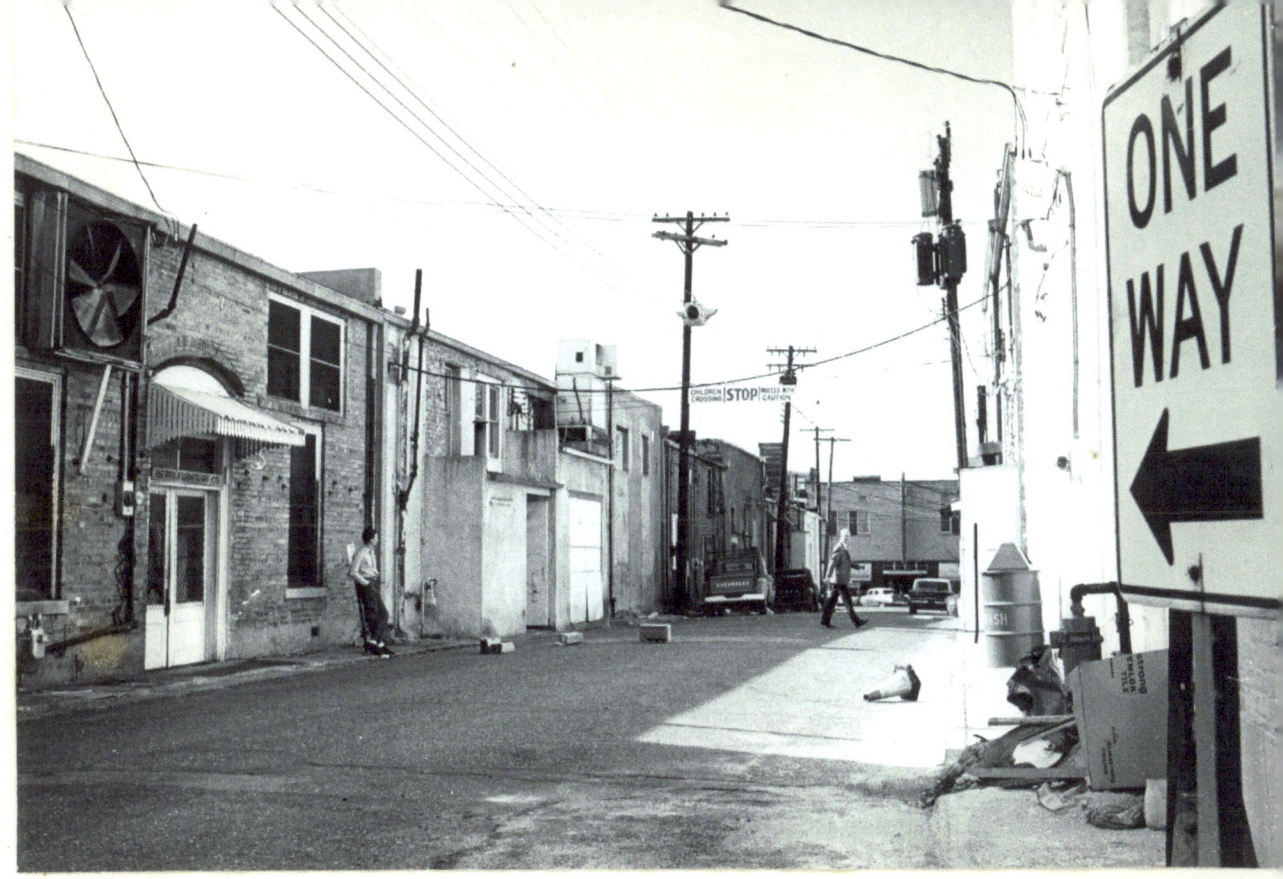

The main street of Ruston bustles with midmorning activity, as
people fall into the fast-moving pace of business in downtown
Ruston.

One of the many famous landmarks which attract tourists, this
one right downtown in easy walking distance of your hotel.

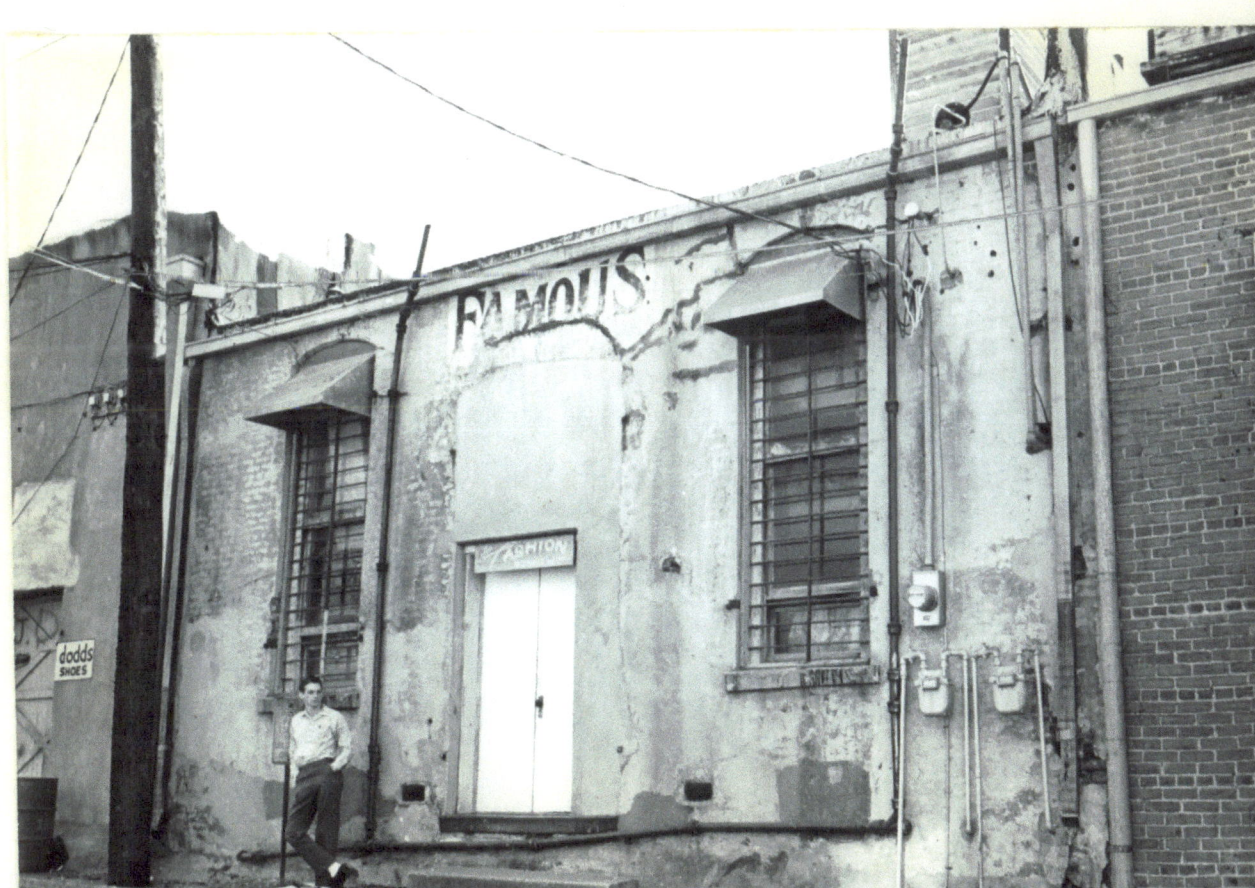

There were several old houses on either side of the railroad tracks between Tech and the center of town. These homes are gone.

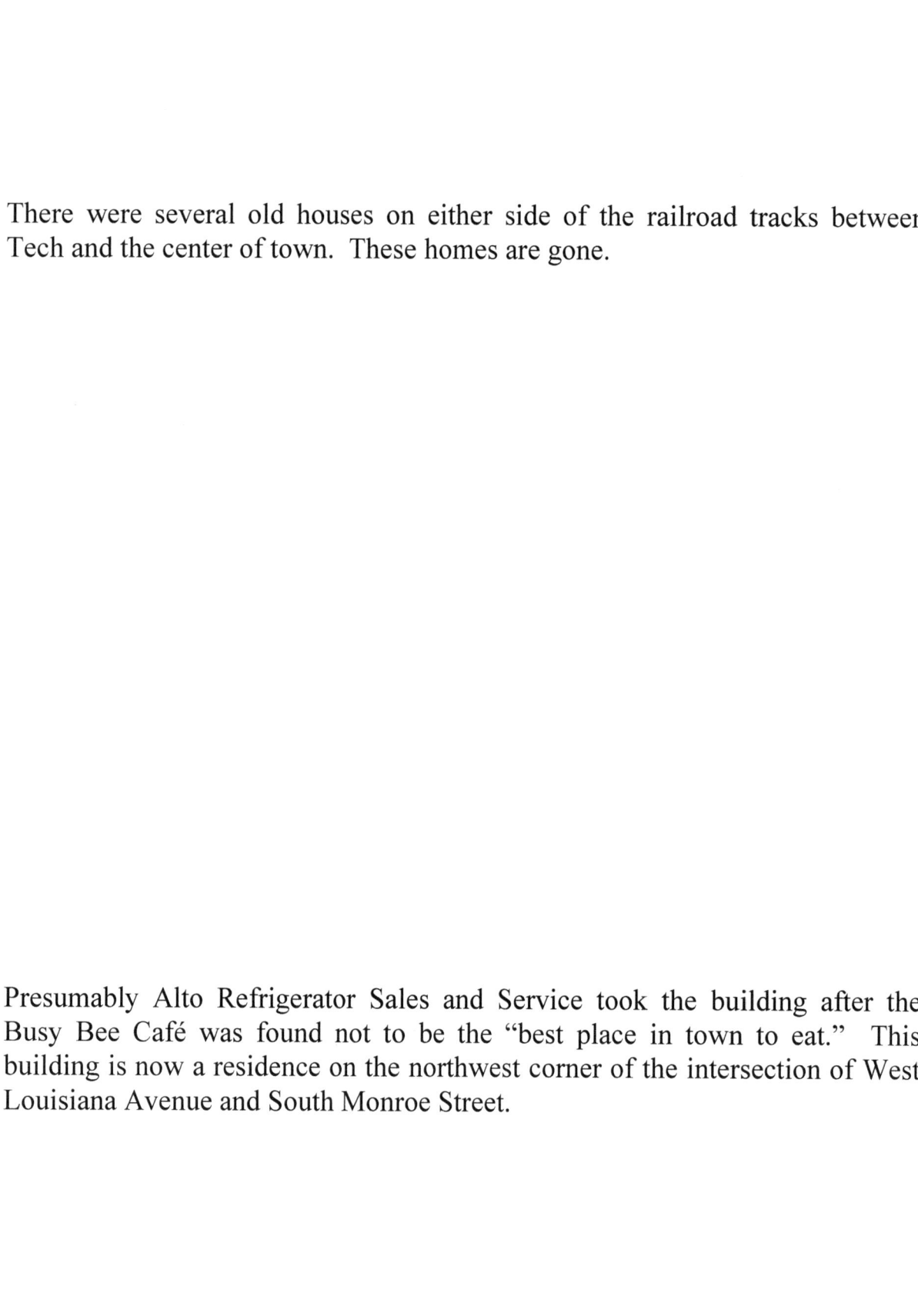

Presumably Alto Refrigerator Sales and Service took the building after the Busy Bee Café was found not to be the "best place in town to eat." This building is now a residence on the northwest corner of the intersection of West Louisiana Avenue and South Monroe Street.

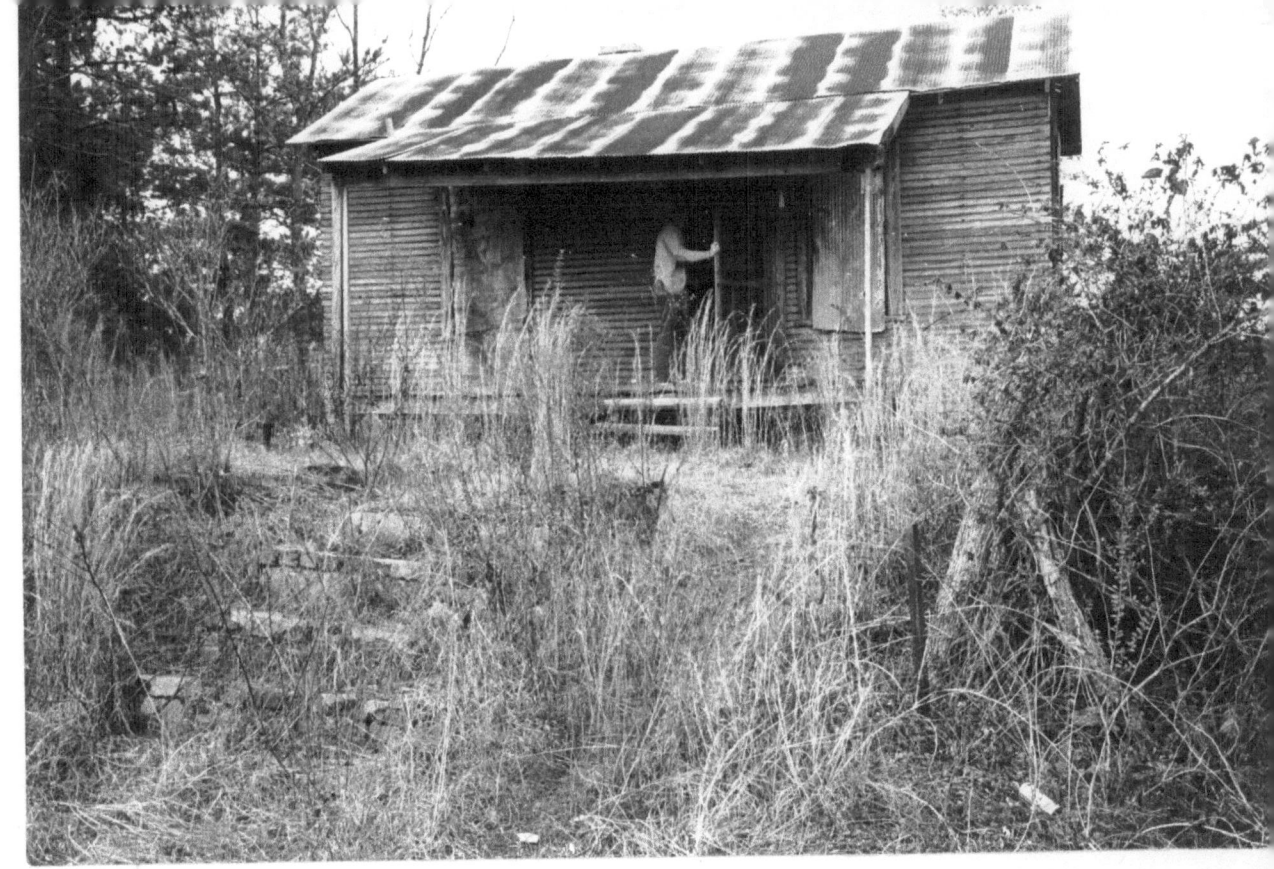

And here is the Ruston Hilton - the largest of the many first
class accommodations in Ruston. Television and cold running
water make staying in the room a veritable pleasure.

For those who enjoy the finest food in the South, this exquisite
dining establishment will certainly provide it.

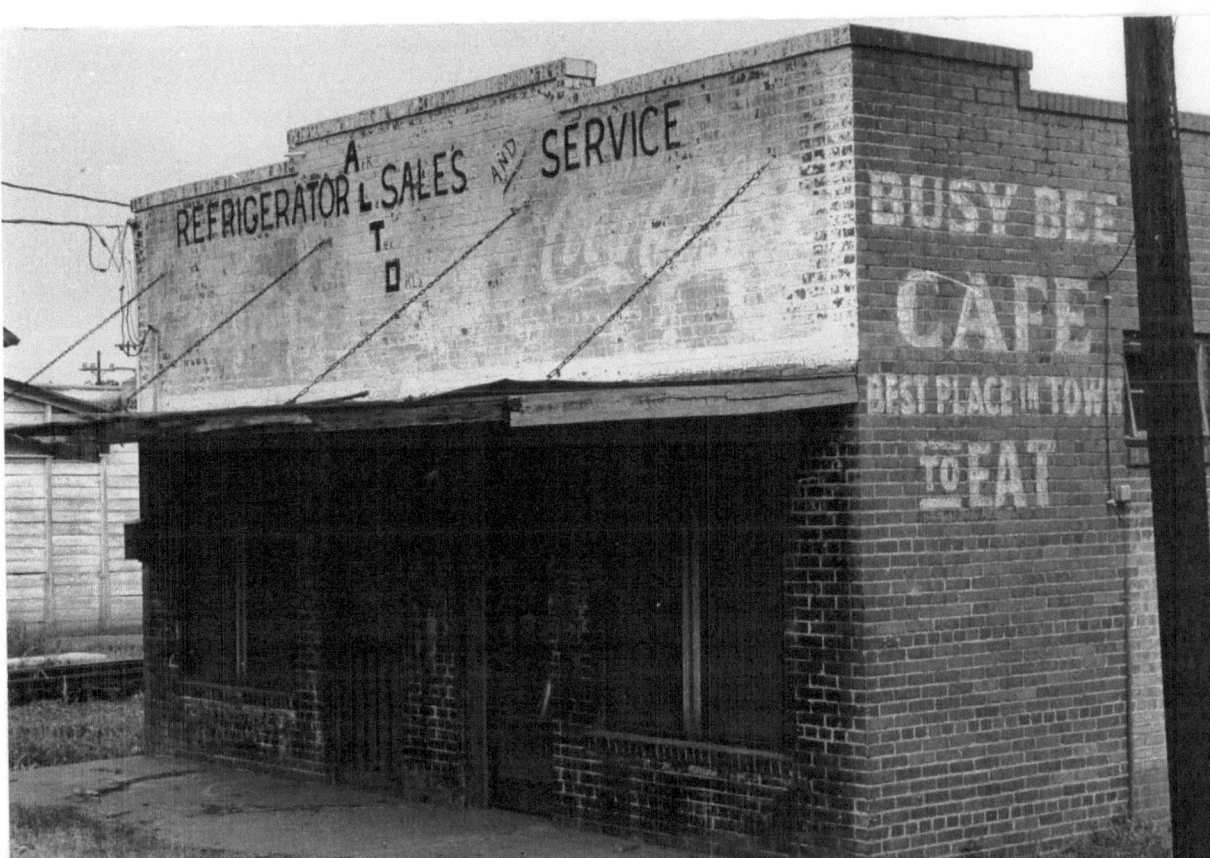

See previous note, top of page 8.

The railroad station and platform are gone, and City Park morphed into Railroad Park. Little Pizzoli's Italian Restaurant occupies the site of the former Ruston Pharmacy across the street.

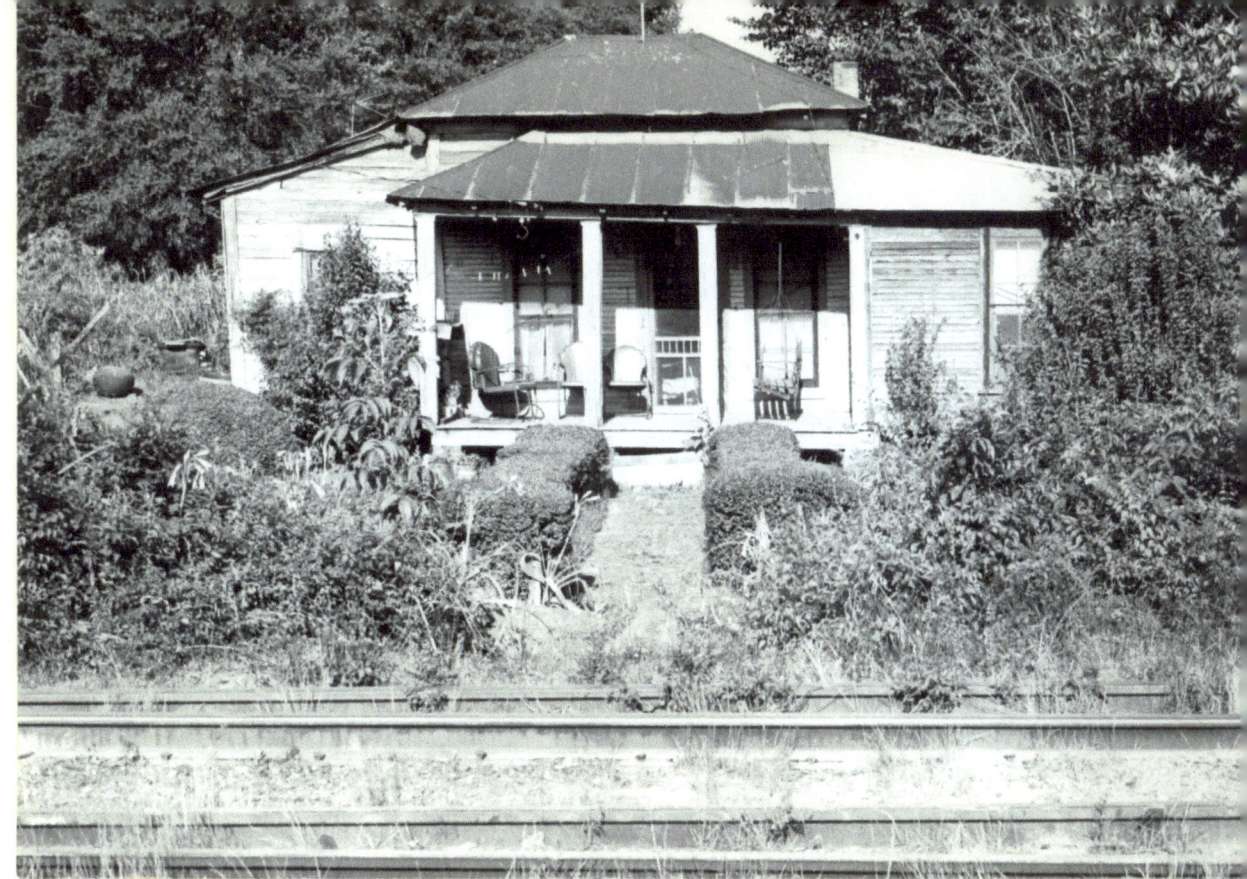

Ruston has its share of Anti-Bellum mansions for which the deep
South is famous. Named Rock Island, this lovely home is found
just off the tracks in the suburbs of town.

Those who prefer the lighter side of life, filled with laughter
and gaiety, will have to visit the broad expansious one-half acre
Ruston City Park for a frollicking Sunday afternoon.

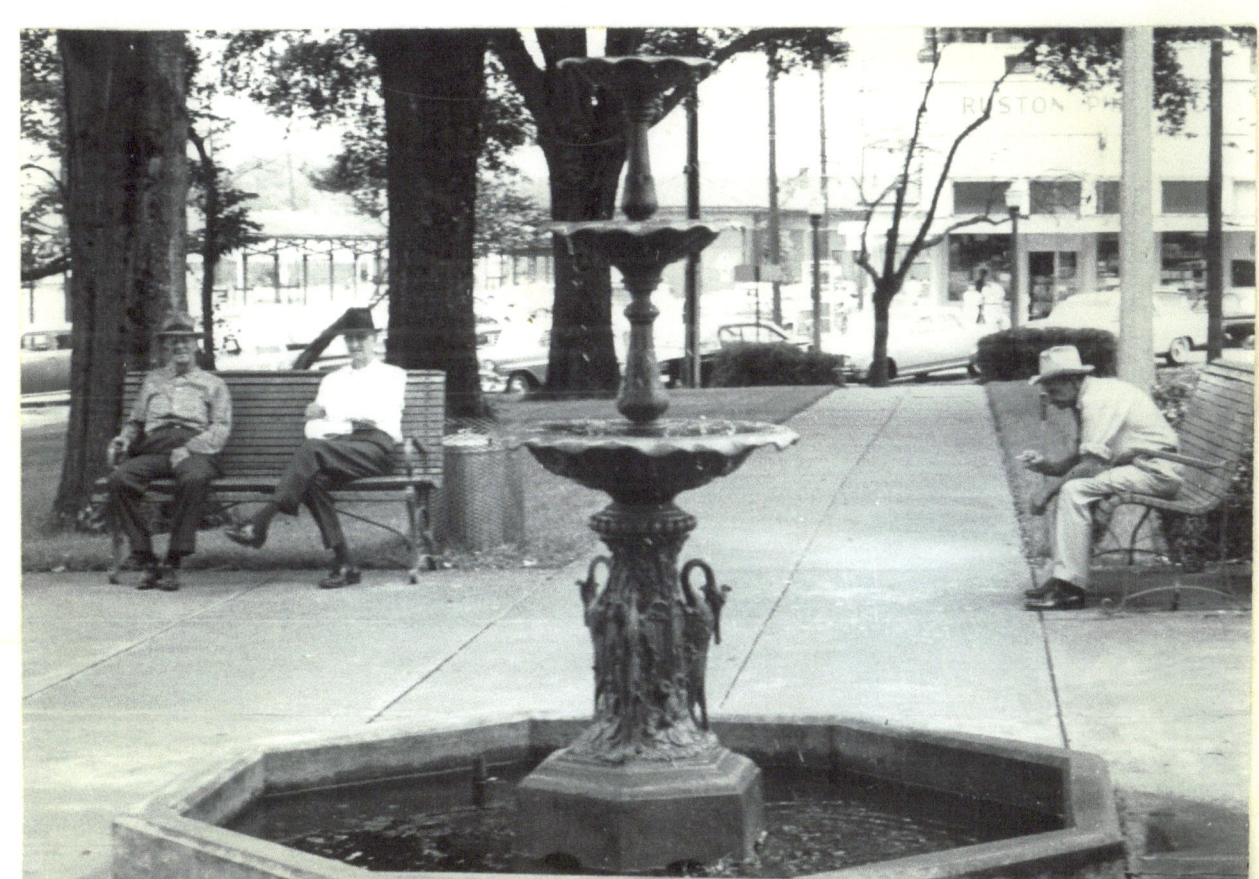

The photo was cropped on the right side. There were no bars in Ruston in the 1960's. LARRY'S BAR was in fact LARRY'S BAR-BQ.

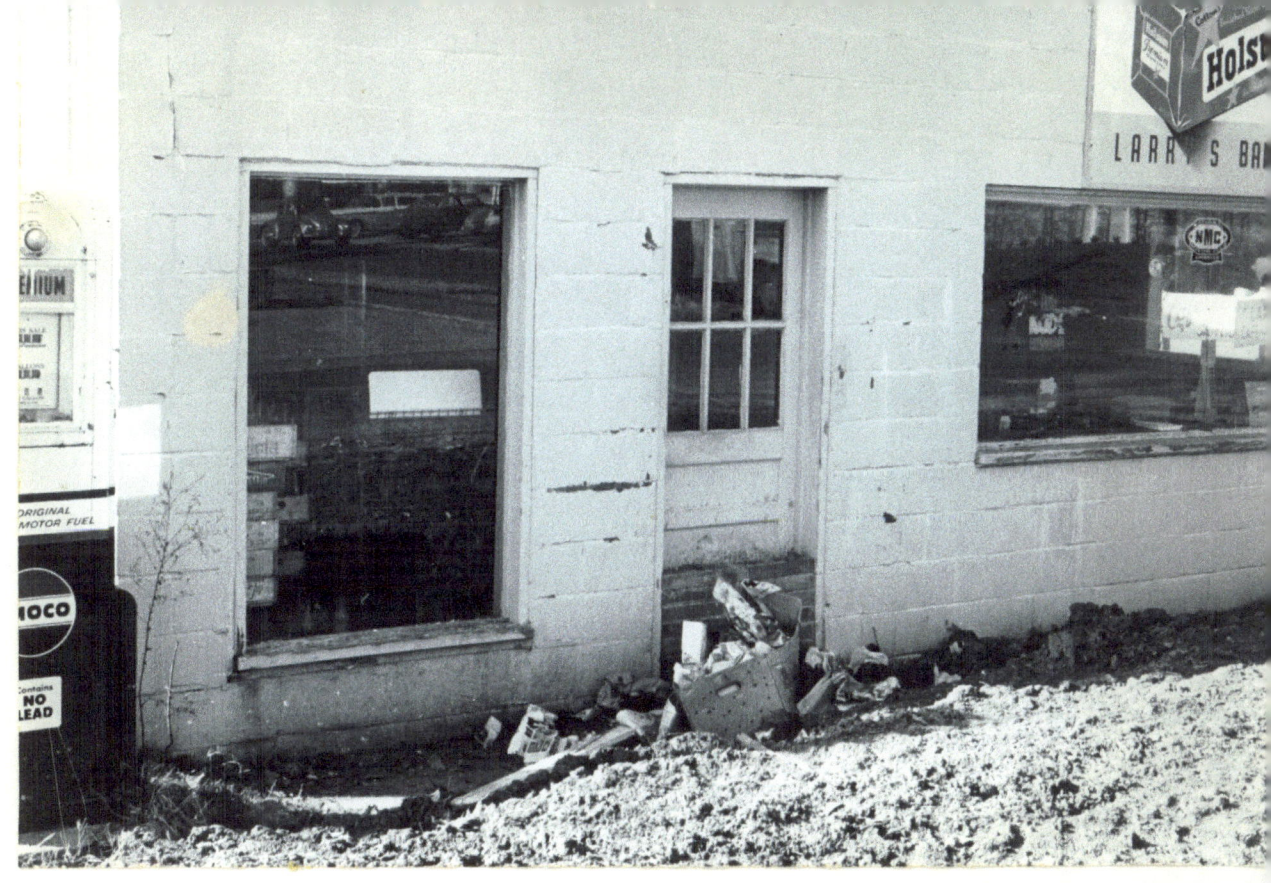

As seen by the sign, this is Larry's Bar, one of the many
sophisticated night spots in metropolitan Ruston.

The Ruston Camping Ground provides clean natural campsites,
untouched by man's influence, for outdoor-minded families.

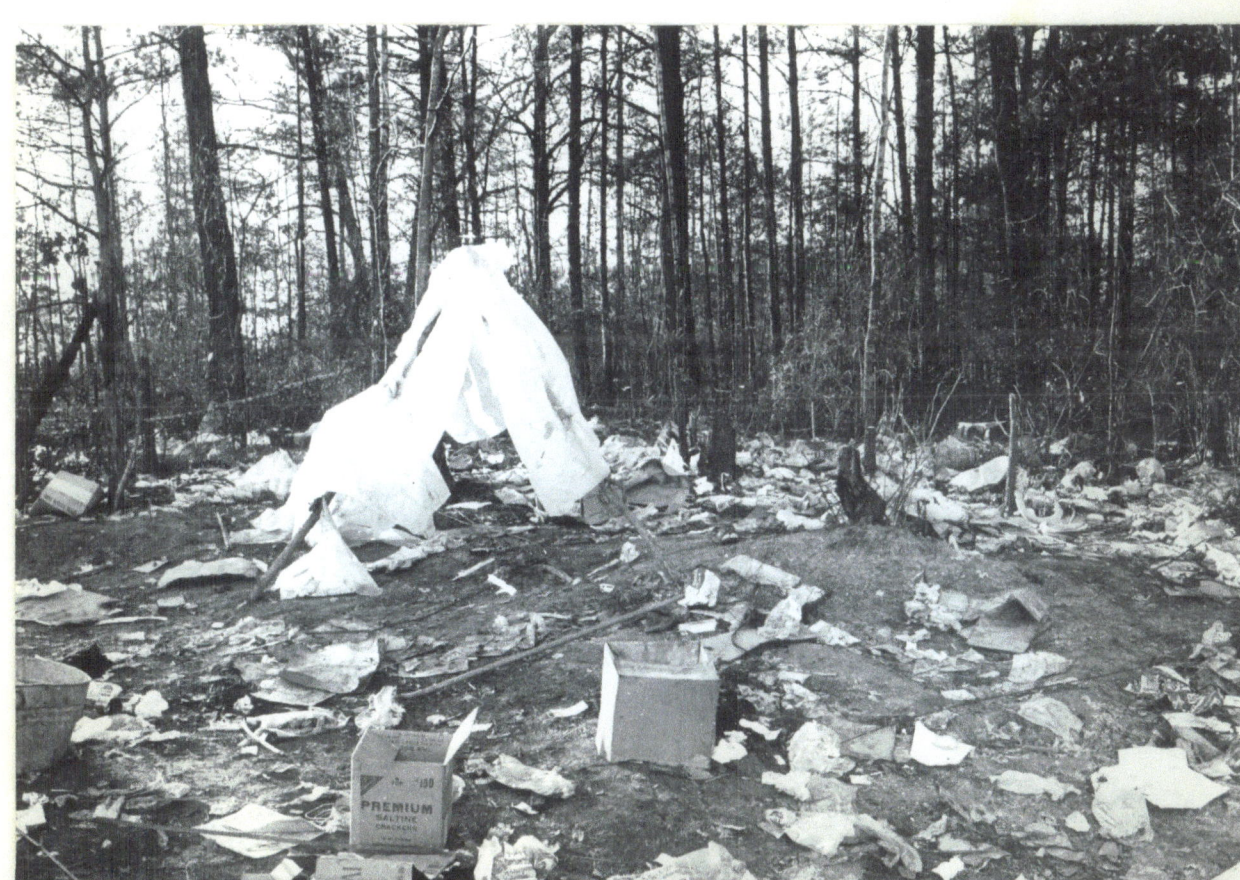

13

A stock pond for watering cattle.

Ruston's landfill practices have probably changed. At the time, trash was burned in the open, metal was reclaimed, and the rest was buried.

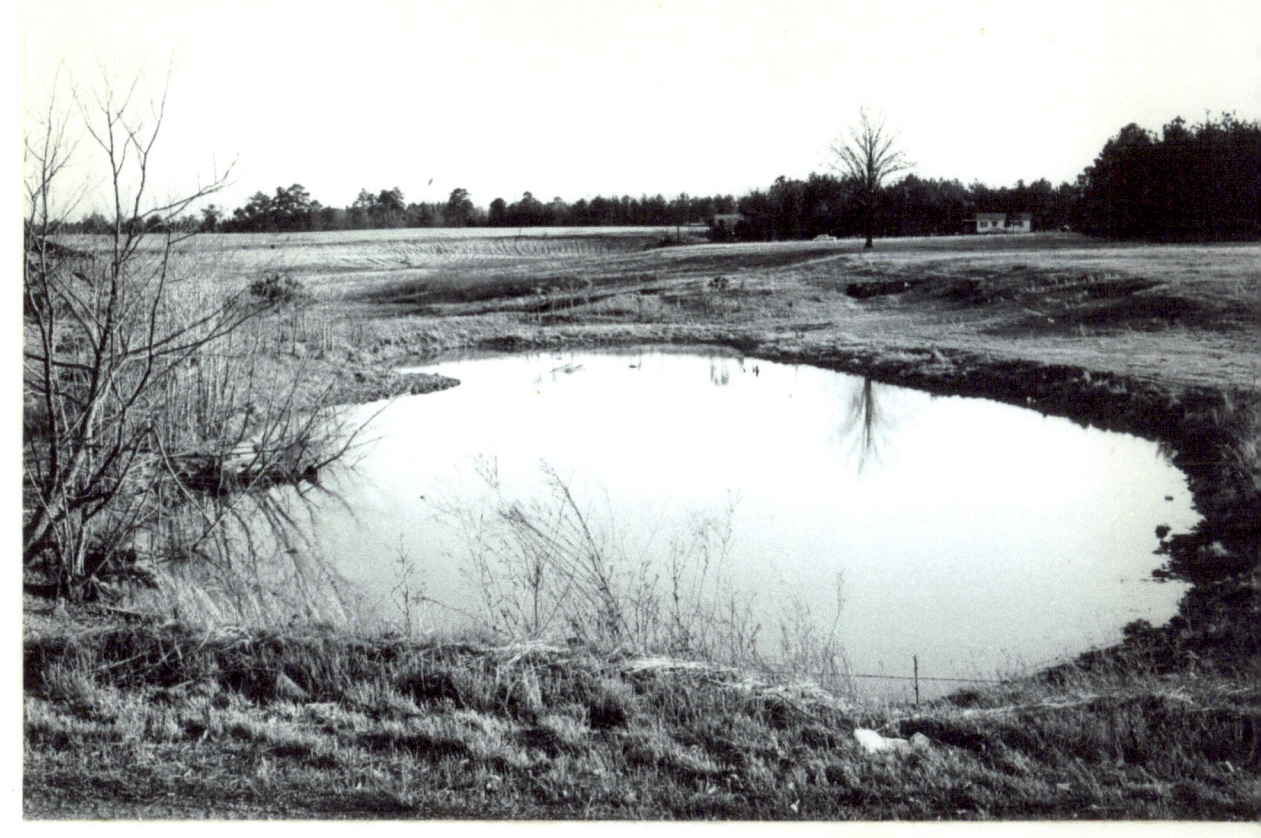

Lake Ruston provides fishing, motor-boating, surf-boarding, and
water-skiing - virtually any water sport. The large lake also
insures that Ruston will have no water shortage.

Neat and spotless picnic areas in Ruston parks are perfect for
"getting away from it all" and enjoying a meal in the cool
surroundings of nature.

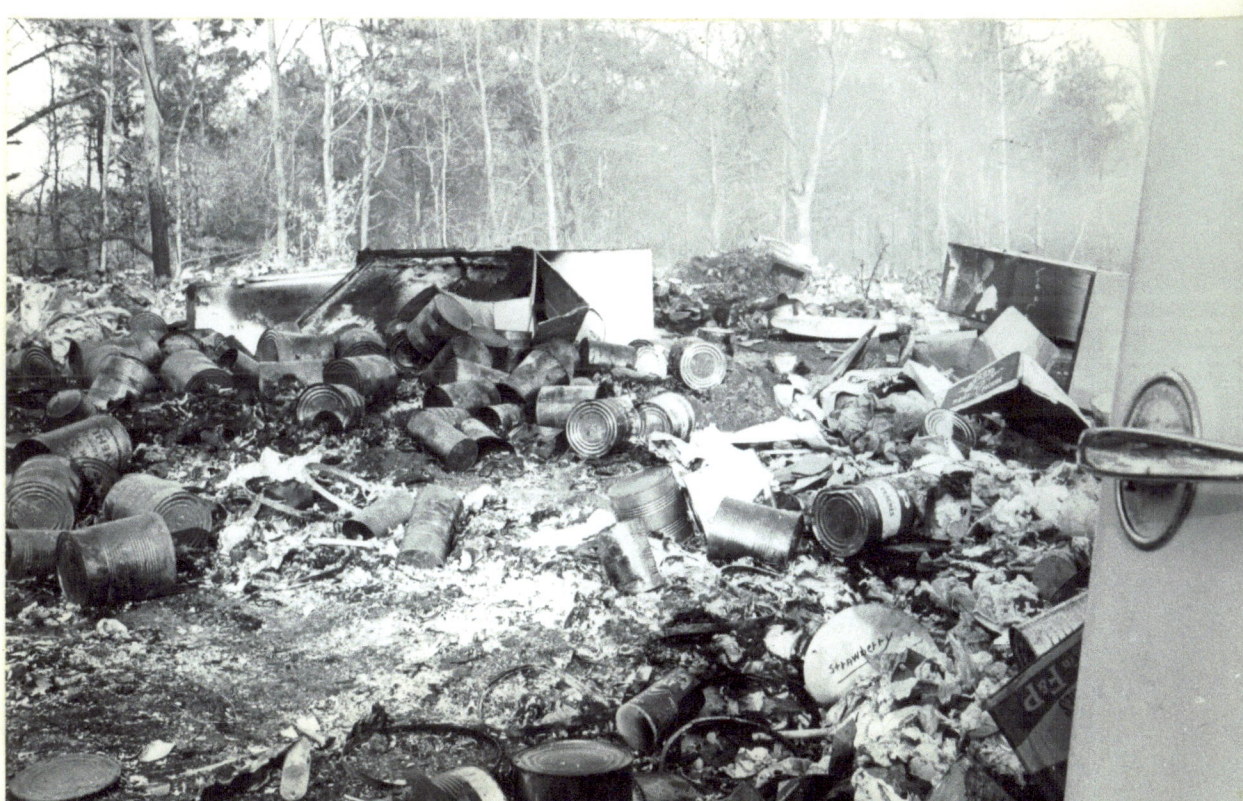

See note, bottom of preceding page.

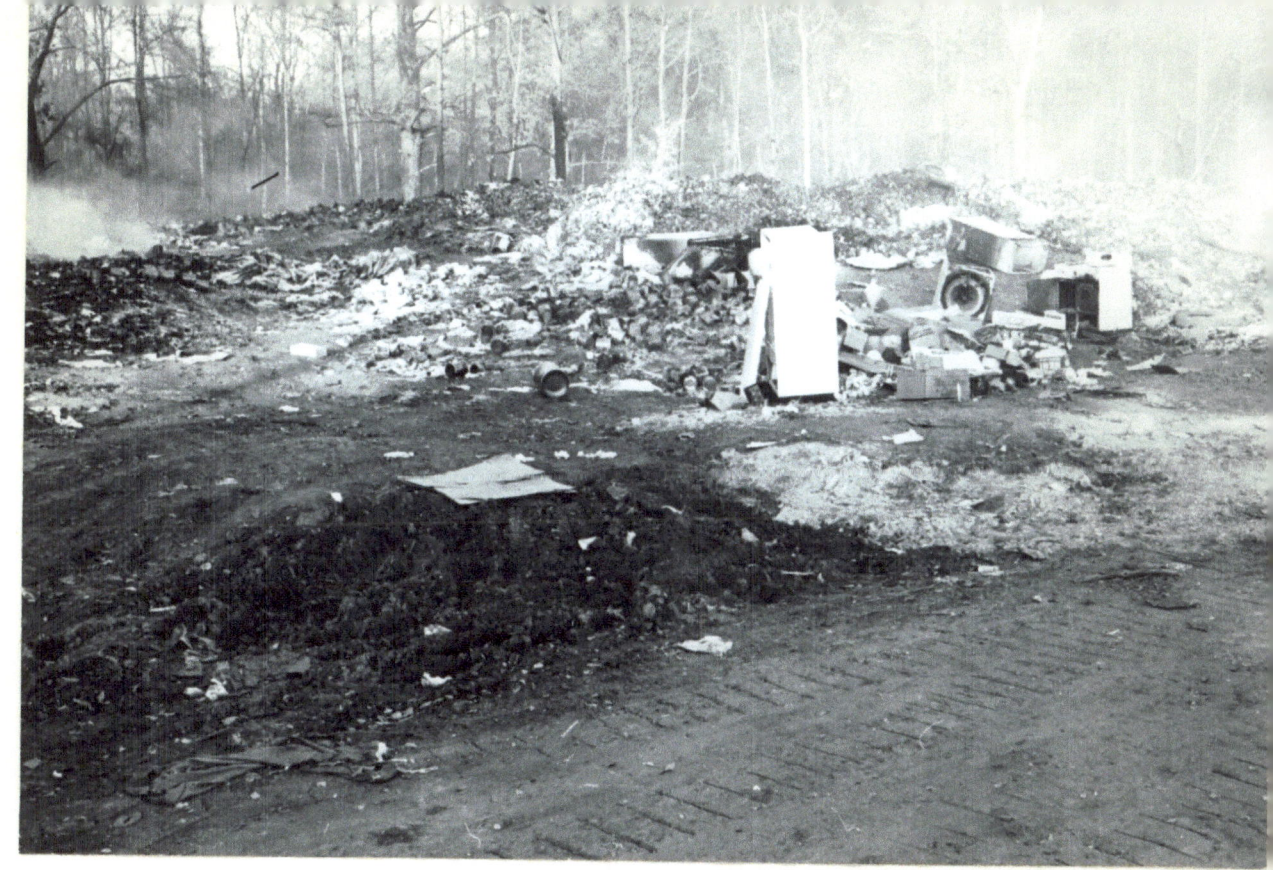

Ruston is noted for its many historical sites and landmarks.
This restoration of Fort Ruston can be seen at the Ruston Civil
War Battleground, where some of the most courageous fighting of
the War occurred.

The Ruston King Ranch has the largest beef herd in North Louisiana. Shown here in its entirety, this herd is worth millions.

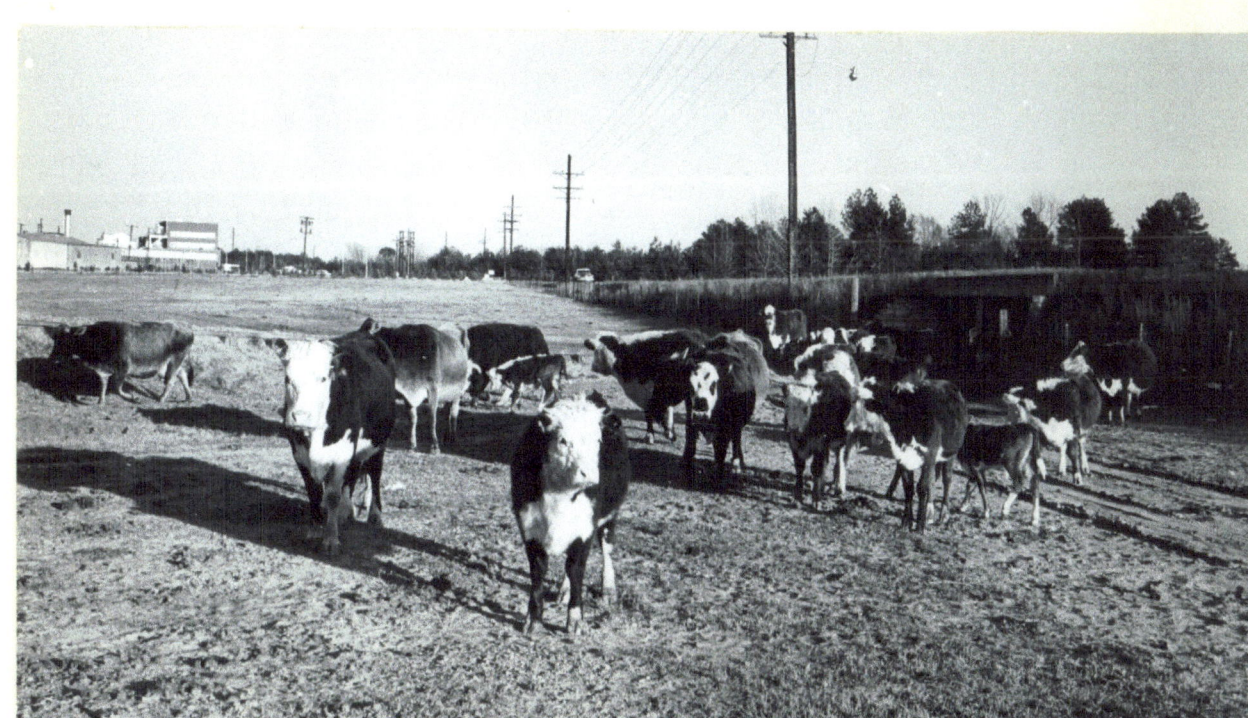

Ruston Brick Works was founded in 1894 and manufactured bricks until 1978. The Beasley family has operated the business since 1947, and continues to distribute building products. The vast diamond and titanium deposits under Ruston remain elusive.

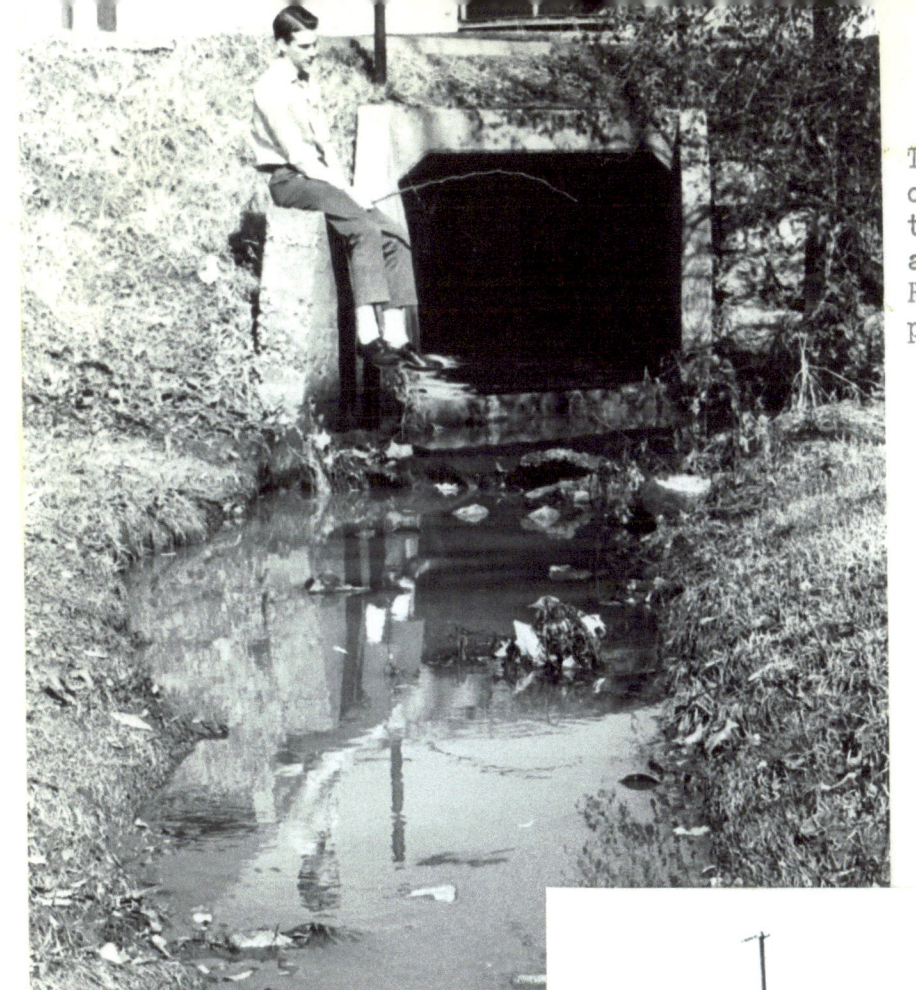

The fast-moving waters of Ruston River, containing many bass, trout, and other fish, makes Ruston a fisherman's paradise.

The entrance of the Ruston Diamond and Titanium Mine is pictured here. This modern up-to-date operation provides employment for thousands of Rustonites.

19

Ruston is located in Lincoln Parish, which was dry in the 1960's. Ouachita Parish was wet and frequently visited by Tech students. The Cheniere Inn (pronounced Shinny In) was located in West Monroe.

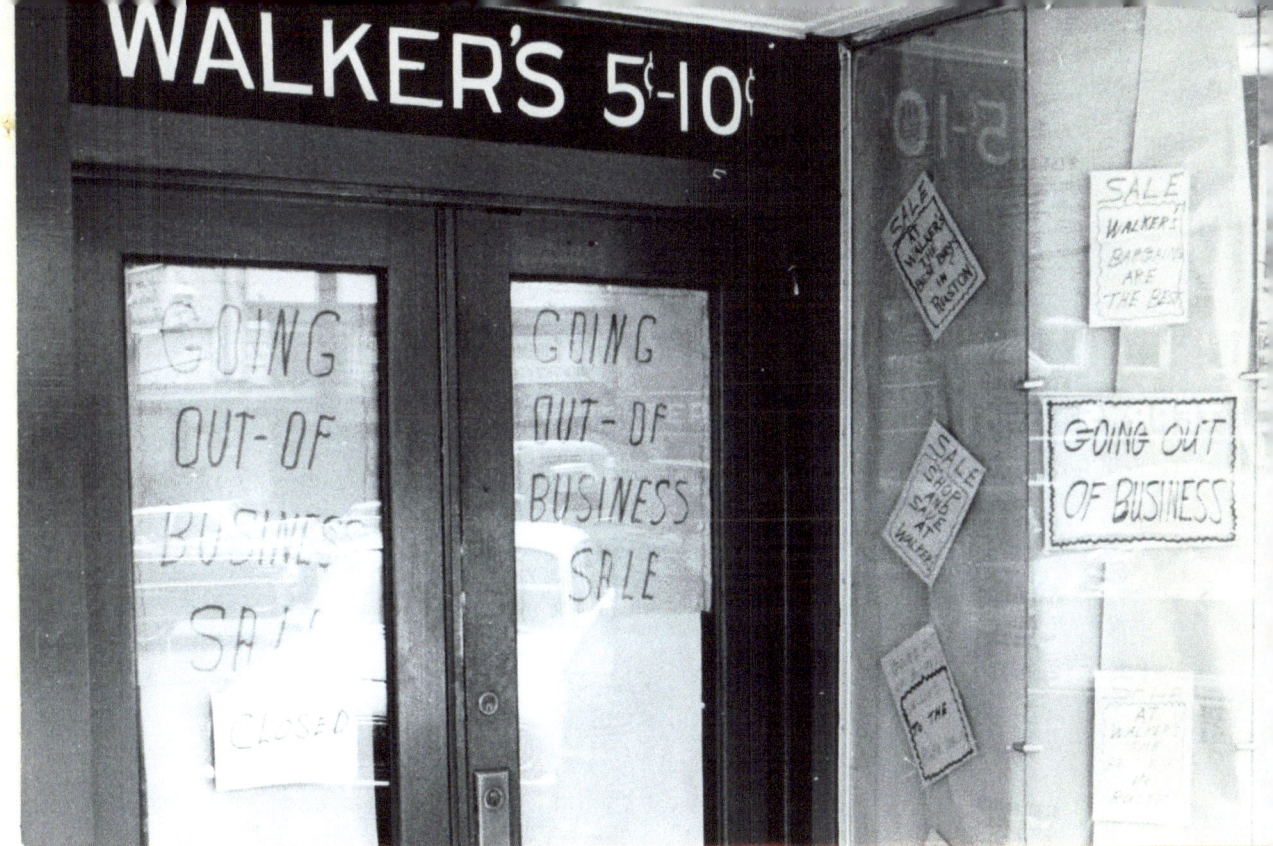

One of Ruston's thriving businesses. The large number of com-
petitive stores in Ruston tends to keep prices at a reasonable
level.

This is another of the outstanding department stores and specialty
shops in the Ruston area. Shopping is a pleasure because of the
amount of high quality merchandise available in stores such as
this.

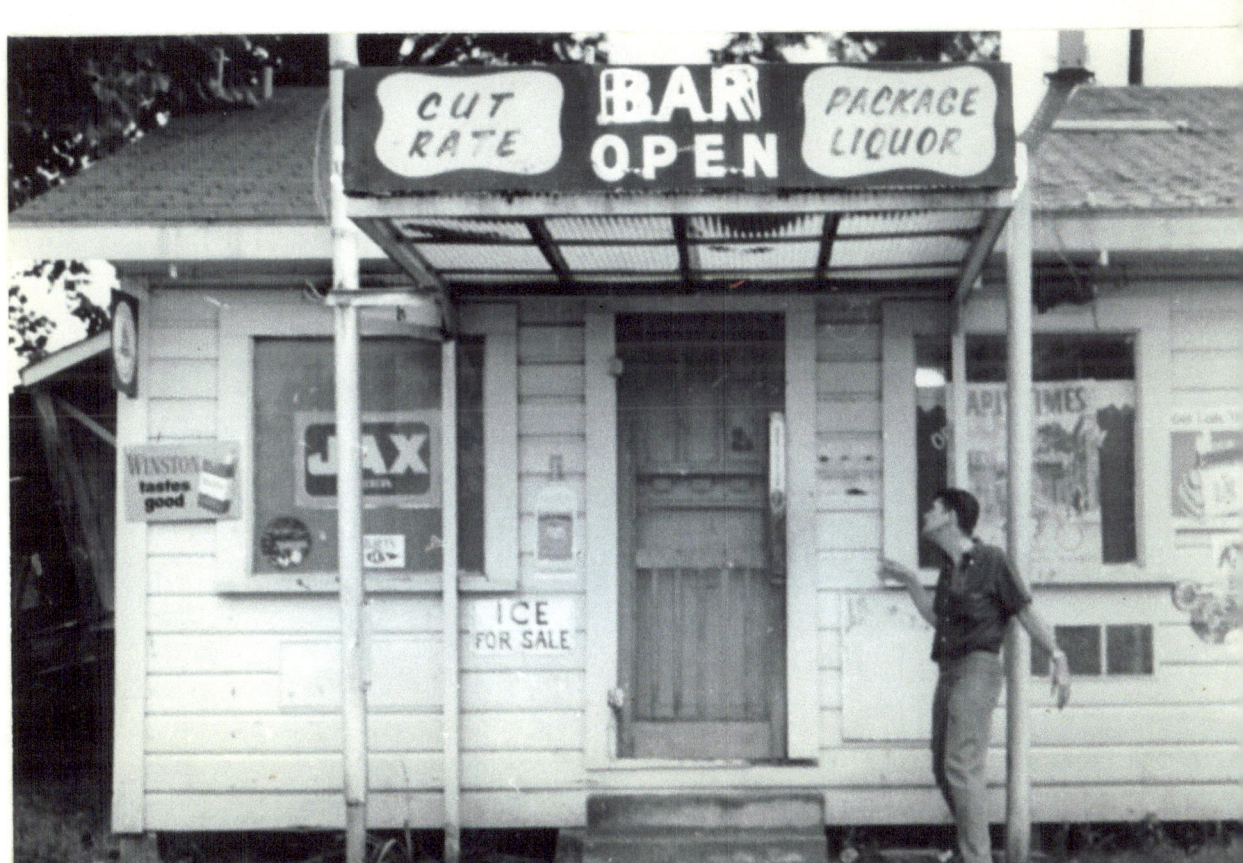

See previous note, bottom of page 18.

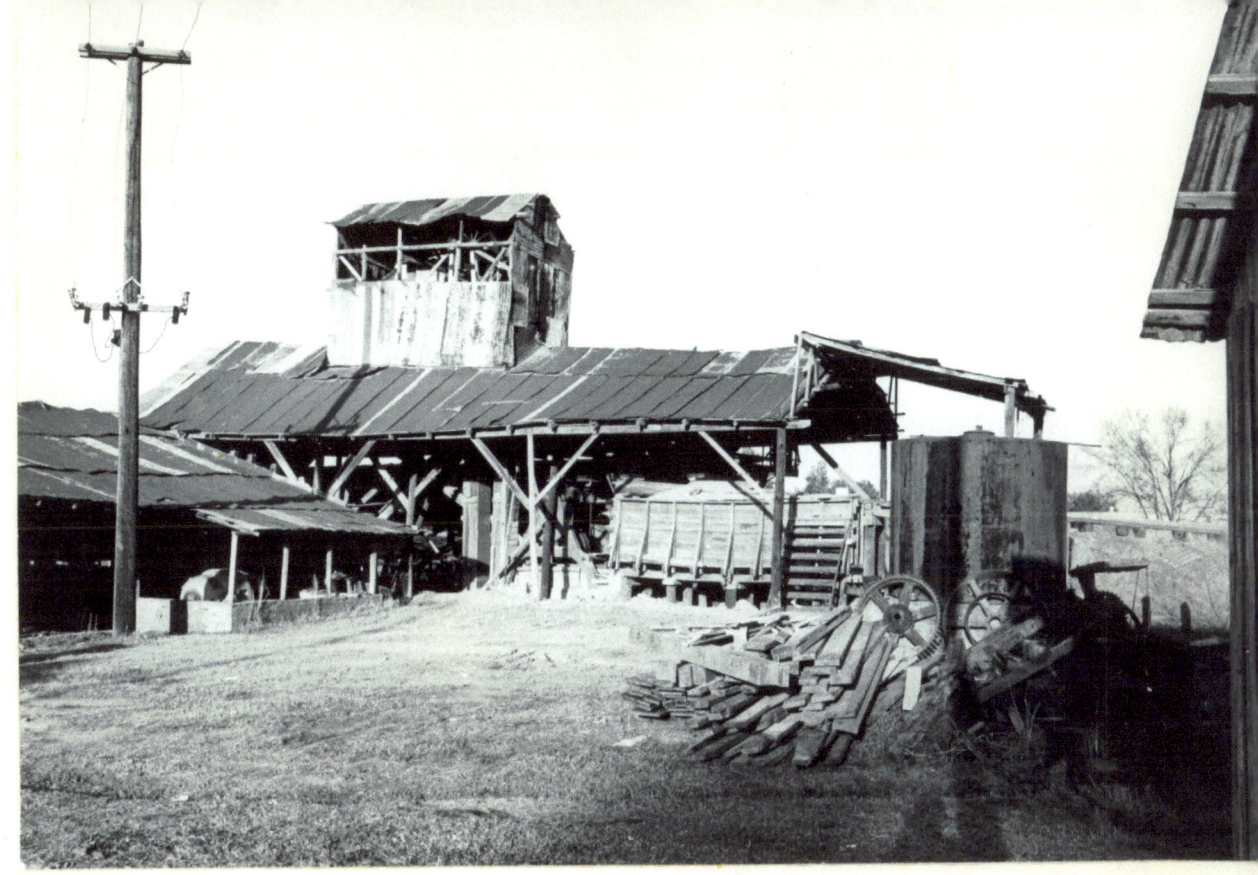

Ruston got electricity in 1962 when this modern power plant was
completed. An engineering marvel, this wood-burning plant is the
only one of its kind in the United States

Ruston has a great deal of room for industrial expansion; this
one-acre plot is located in one of the most beautiful parts of town.

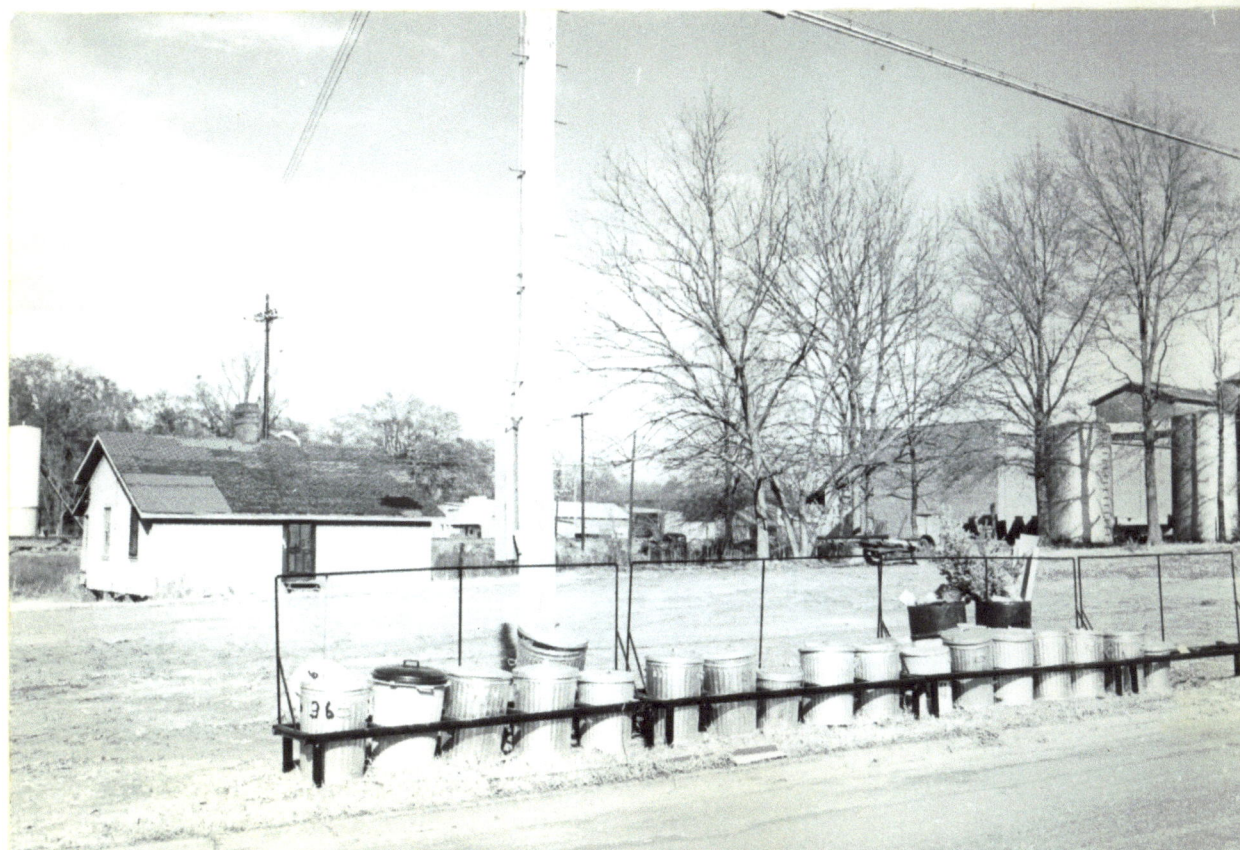

23

Ruston Municipal Airport dated to the 1930's but the city outgrew it. Ruston Regional Airport was built with a longer runway, a few miles southeast of town. The old runway is used by the Ruston Police Department for vehicle chase training, and nearby ground serves as athletic fields. The former airport office is now a church, and the aircraft hangar is gone. The row of chairs paralleled the runway, and were a comfortable vantage point for pilots not flying to critique takeoffs and landings of pilots who were.

Half a century later, this Piper J-3 Cub aircraft N1459N is airworthy, and is based at Anoka County-Blaine Airport near Minneapolis.

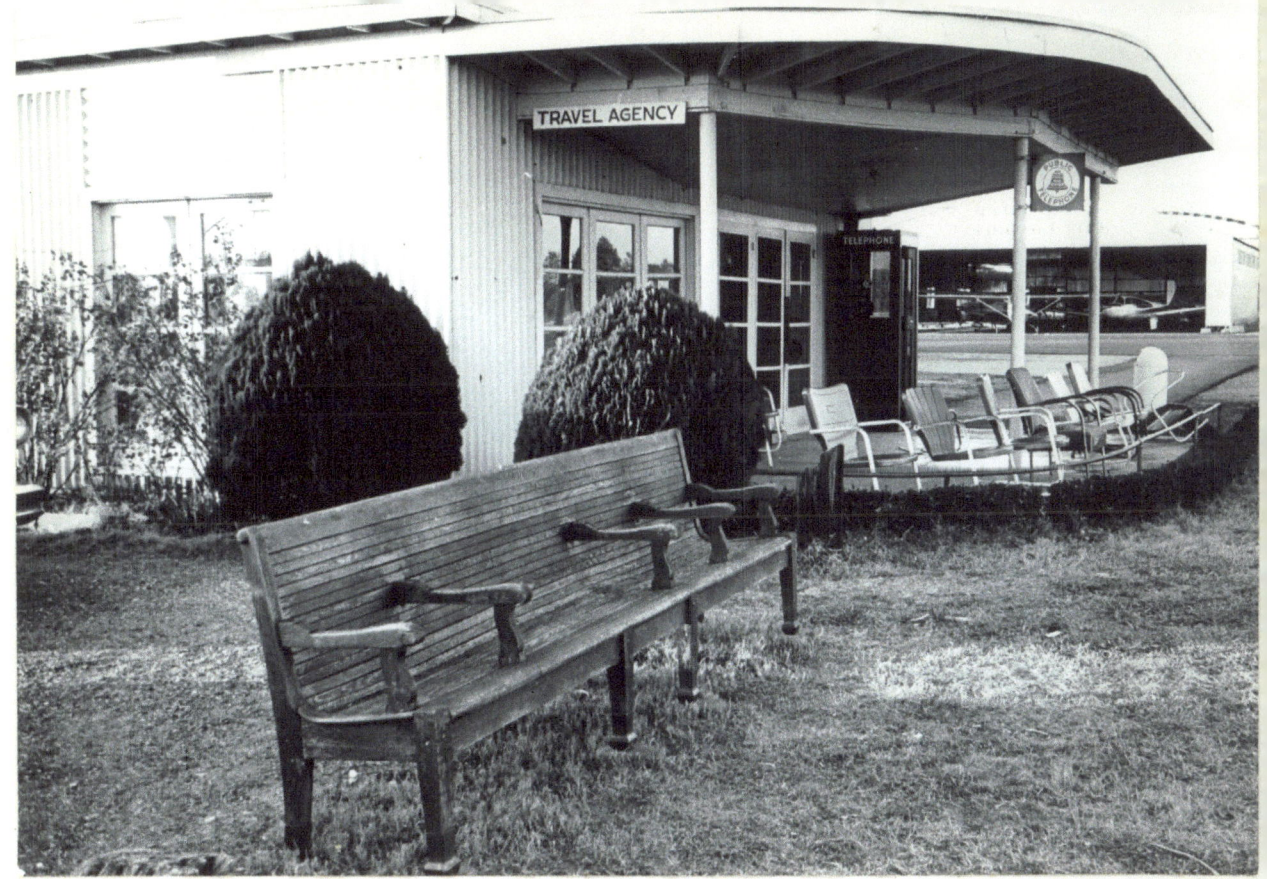

The terminal of Ruston International Airport is second only to
Dallas Love Field in traffic handling in the Southwest. Some
people also come to Ruston through this airport.

A fighter pilot starts his slim supersonic aircraft at the Ruston
Strategic Air Command Base.

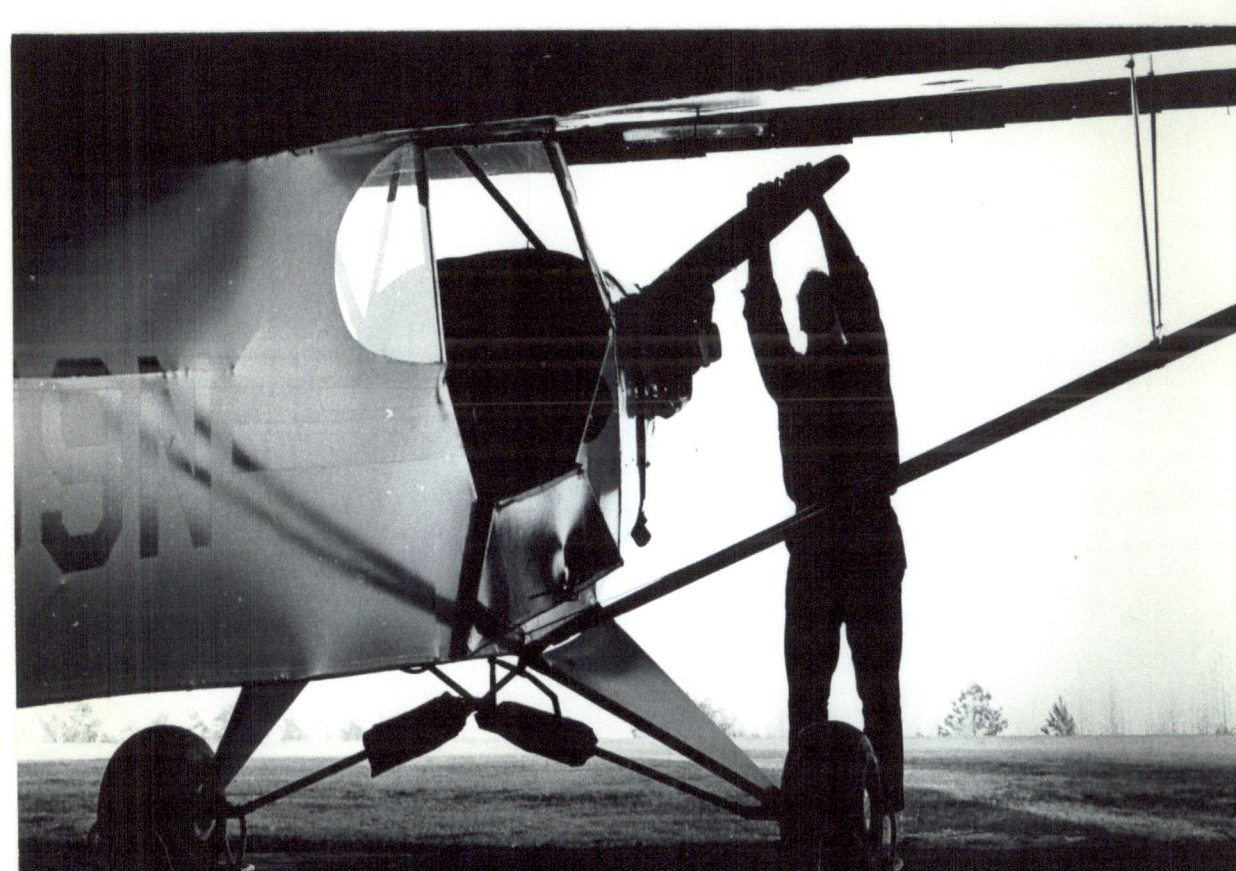

U. S. Navy trainees occupied these barracks during World War Two. They survive at Tech, having housed biomedical and nuclear research activities.

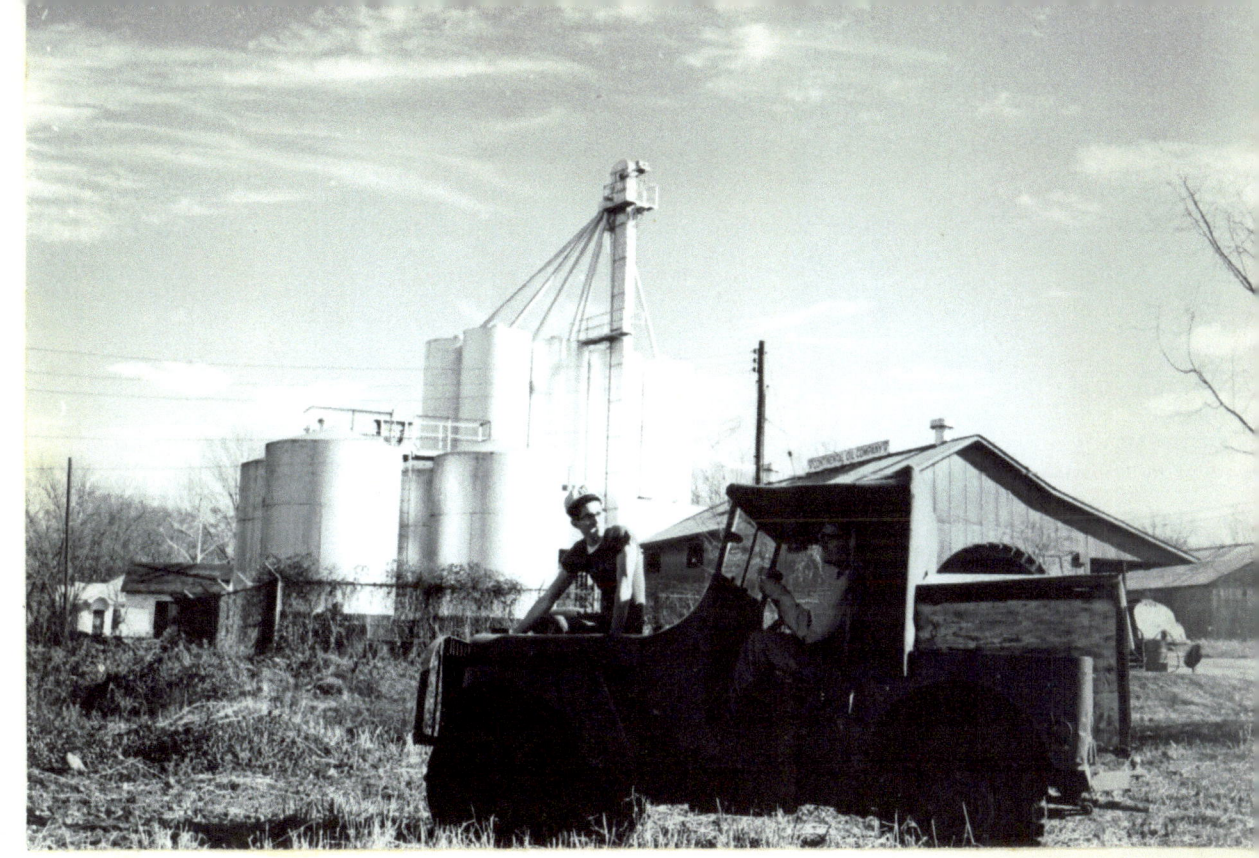

One of the many industrial complexes which offer business and
employment in Ruston.

Ruston has set national standards in educational excellence.
Louisiana Tech is contained in this modernistic 20 room World
War II barracks which houses 400 men and 298 women students.

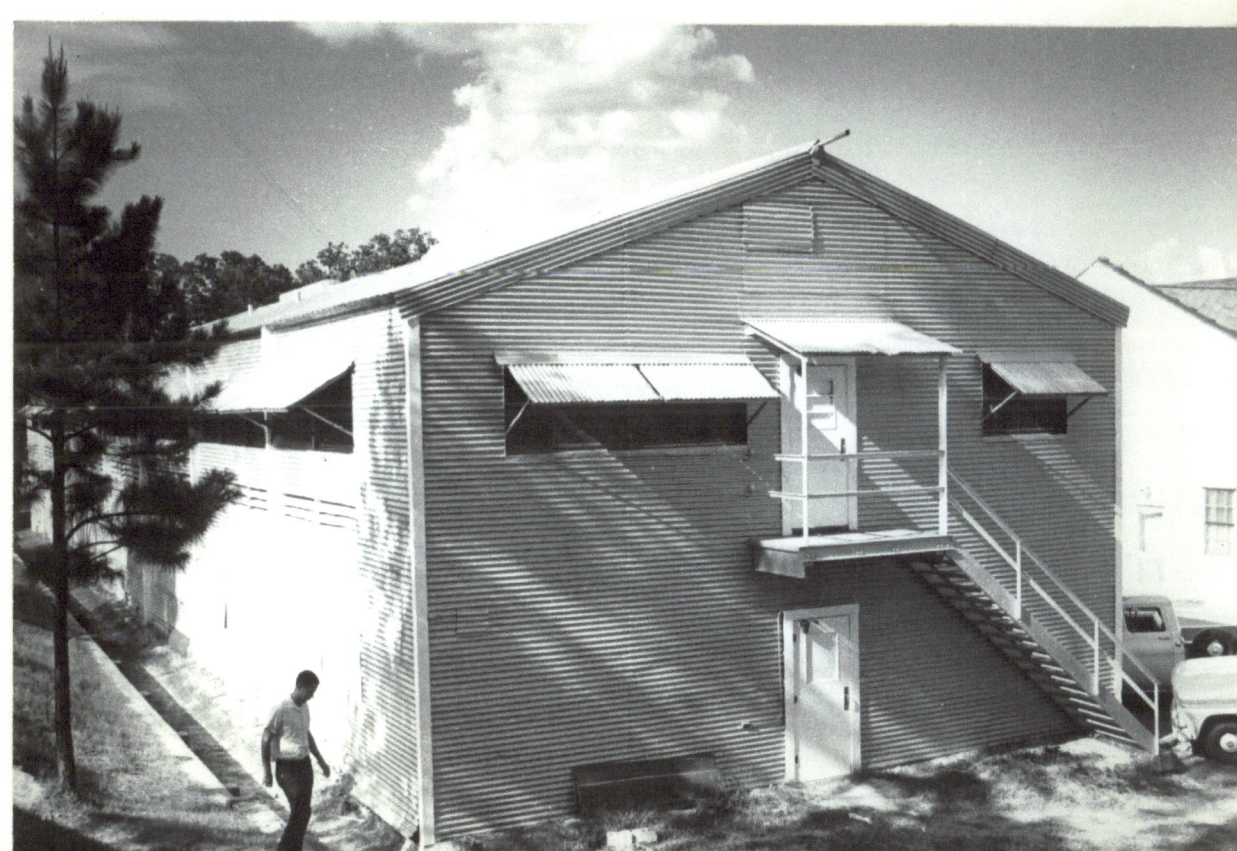

The *Ruston Daily Leader* newspaper now occupies this building at 212 West Park Avenue. The sign referred to the Harris Hospital and Café, which was just across the parking lot to the east.

Greenwood Cemetery

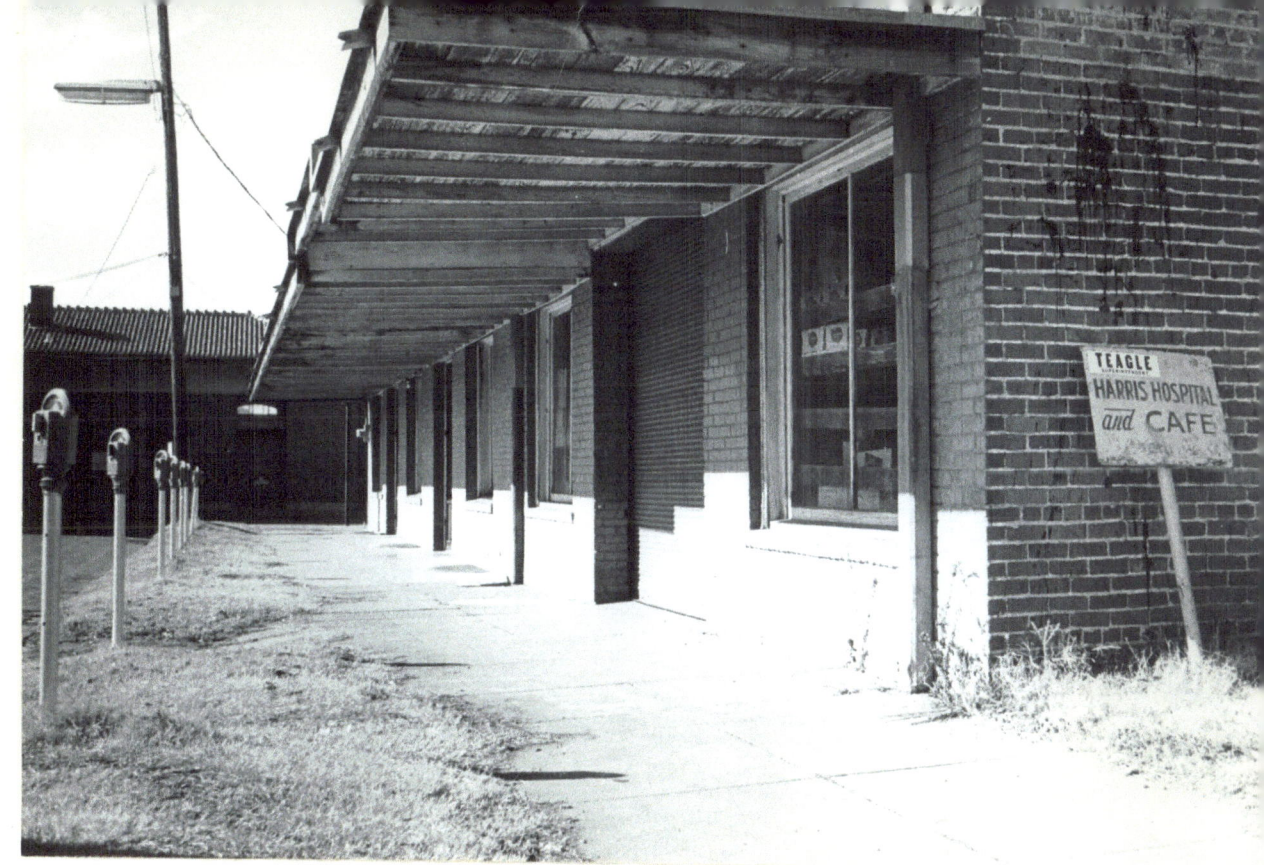

The Harris Hospital and Cafe is one of the leading clinics in
the nation. Its 13 beds and indoor conveniences make it the best
hospital in the region.

This is the entrance to the Marble Hill Home for the Aged,
where Ruston retires her senior citizens.

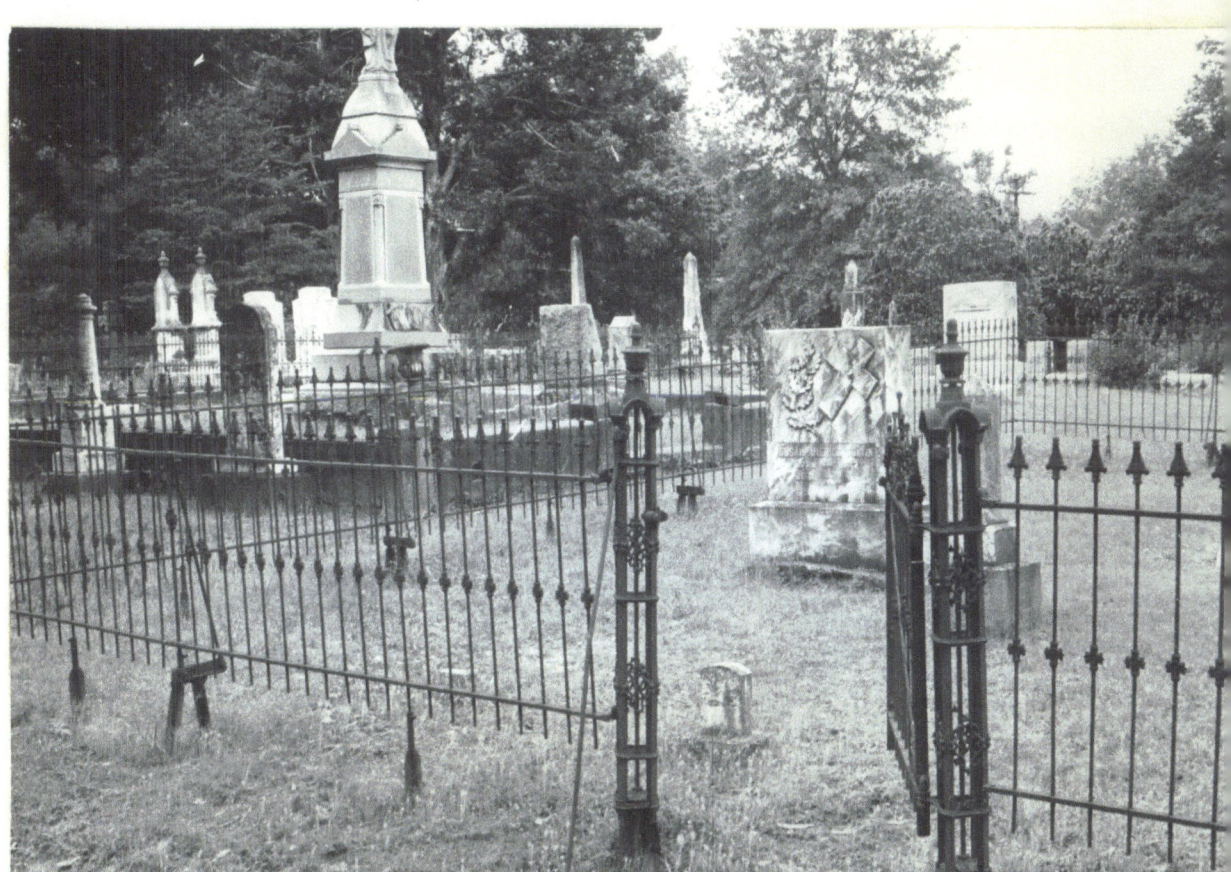

The railroad station is gone and Ruston is no longer a depot stop.

See previous note, bottom of page 20.

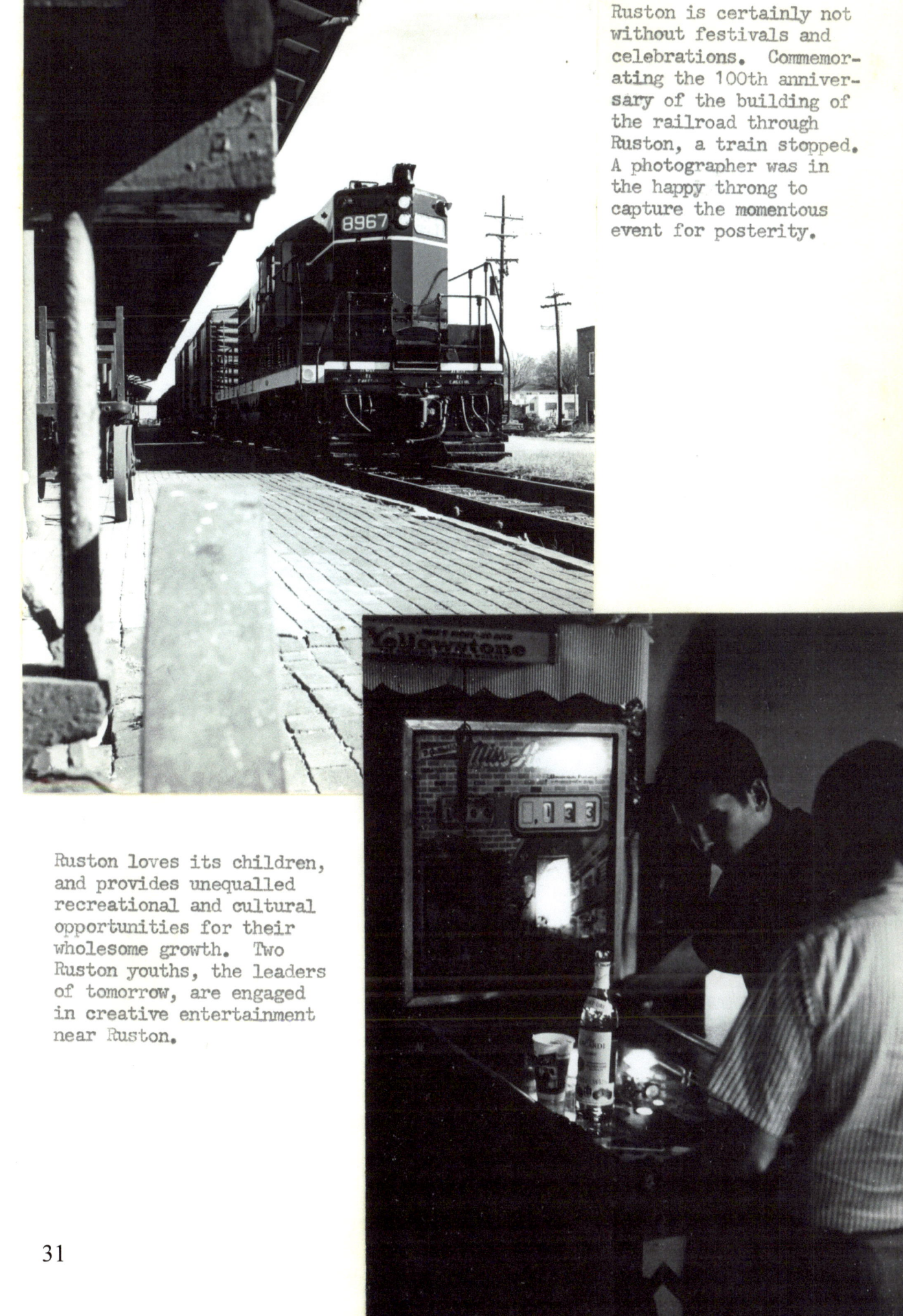

Ruston is certainly not without festivals and celebrations. Commemorating the 100th anniversary of the building of the railroad through Ruston, a train stopped. A photographer was in the happy throng to capture the momentous event for posterity.

Ruston loves its children, and provides unequalled recreational and cultural opportunities for their wholesome growth. Two Ruston youths, the leaders of tomorrow, are engaged in creative entertainment near Ruston.

31

What could better fit the needs of college students?

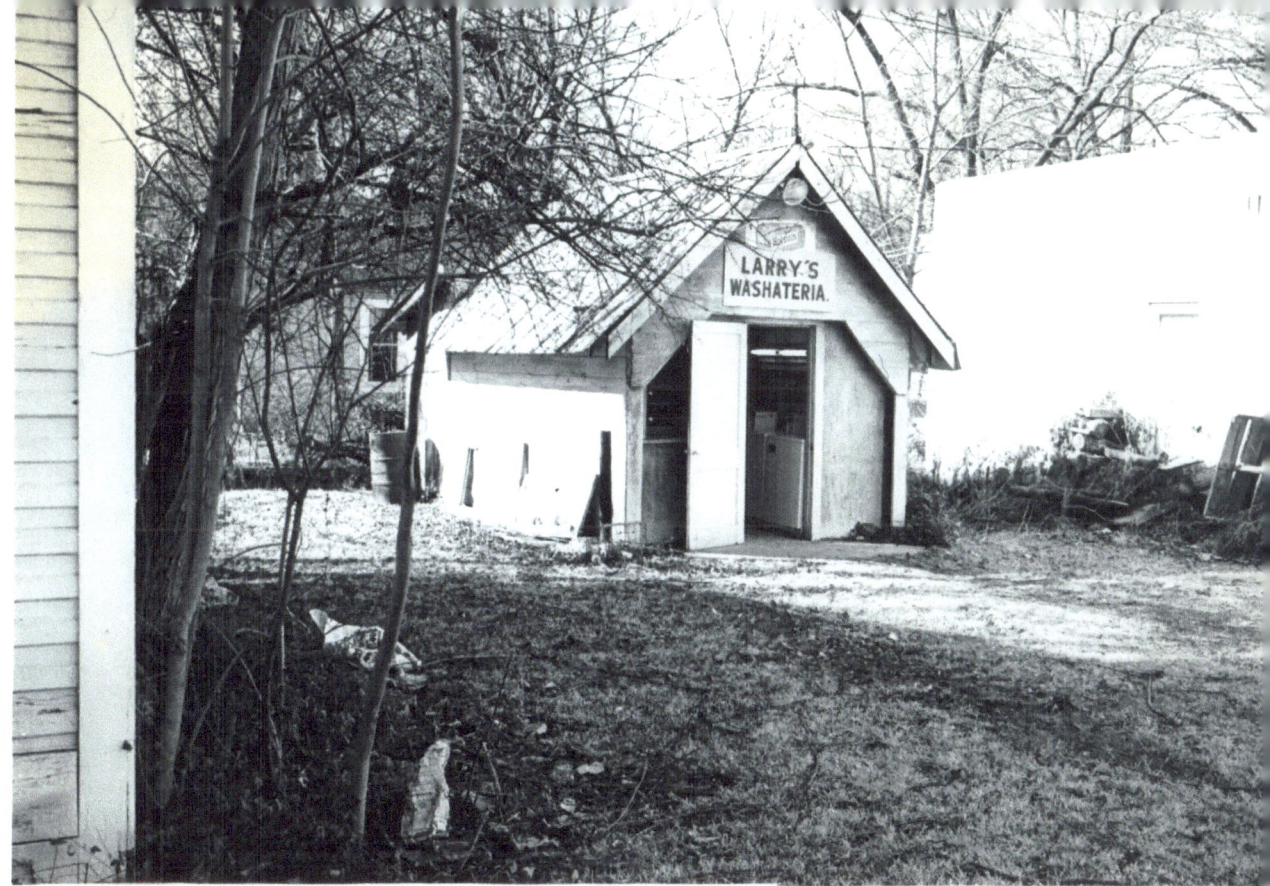

Untitled

The author hitchhiked home to Sulphur a couple of times, and does not recommend it. He also remembers the notorious speed trap in the picturesque village of Dry Prong, Louisiana.

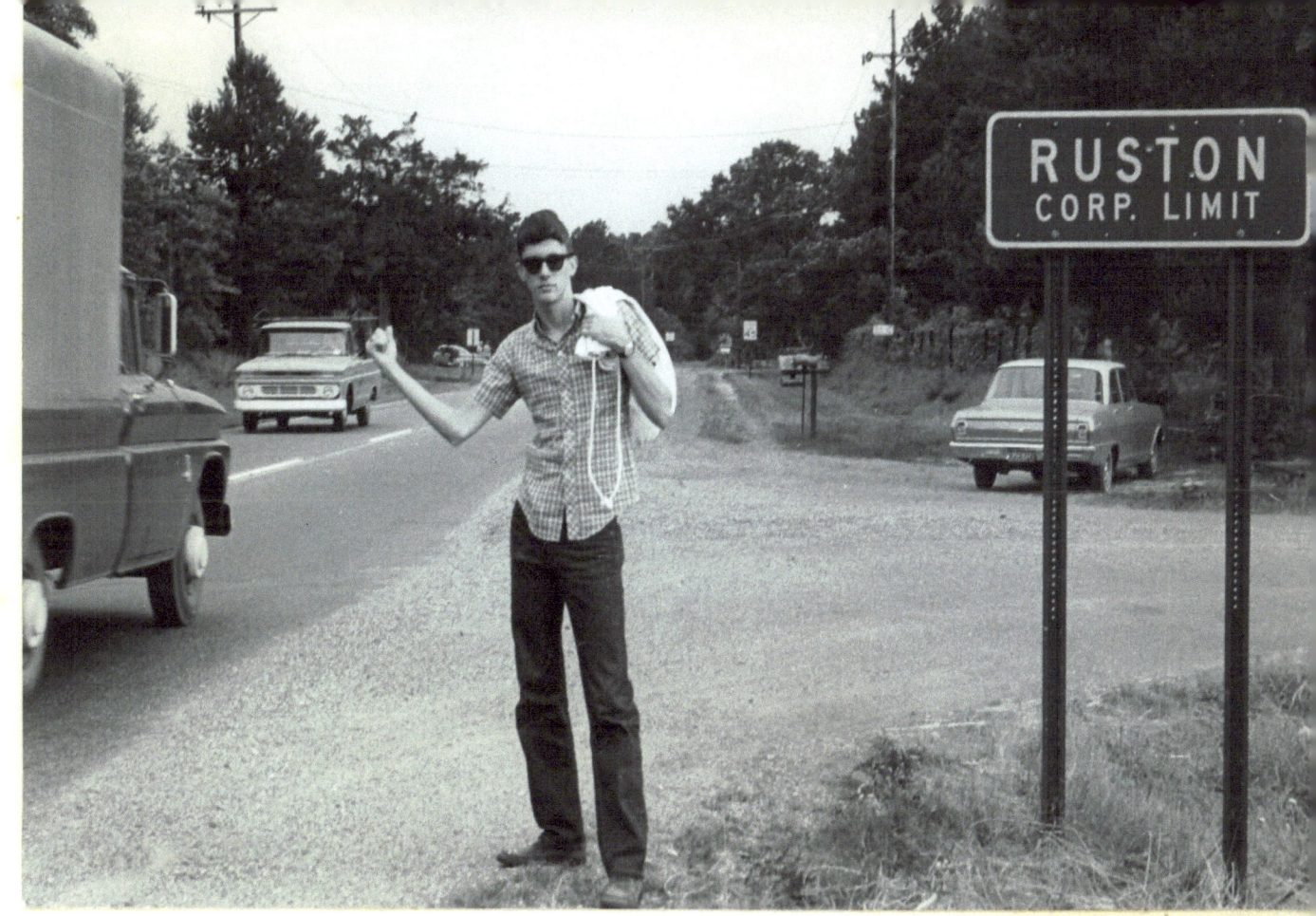

You will find it hard to leave Ruston; the friendlest town in
the South, where people shake your hand and ask, "How did you
happen to be in Ruston?" But come back to scenic Ruston - a
wonderful place to live.

ABOUT THE IMAGES

The photographs were taken with a Minolta SR-3 35mm single lens reflex camera with a 55mm normal lens, shooting Kodak Plus-X pan film. They were developed and printed in the darkroom at Tech Studio, under the staircase in Keeny Hall.

ABOUT THE AUTHOR

John Wood, seen in the opening and closing images, grew up in Southwestern Louisiana. His family moved to an oil refinery town after World War Two and he graduated from Sulphur High School in 1961. John attended Louisiana Tech from 1961 to 1965, graduating with a bachelor's degree in electrical engineering. He worked summers at Texas Instruments in Dallas. John moved to Boston and attended Massachusetts Institute of Technology, graduating with a master's degree in electrical engineering in 1967. He spent much of his career in the management and leadership of high technology businesses, including roles as public company CEO. John now serves on corporate boards and lives with his wife in Concord, Massachusetts. He received the Distinguished Alumnus Award from the Louisiana Tech University College of Engineering and Science in 1996.

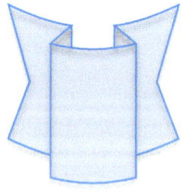